FOR JULIA & LAURA

BREAD REVOLUTION

RISE UP & BAKE

**Duncan Glendinning
& Patrick Ryan**

MURDOCH BOOKS

CONTENTS

PATRICK

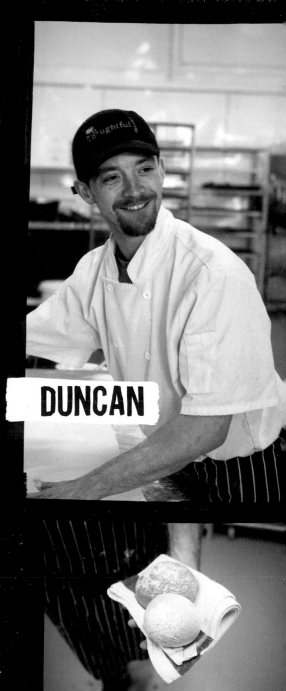

DUNCAN

JOIN THE BREAD REVOLUTION!

'Bread is the king of the table and all else is merely the court that surrounds the king. The countries are the soup, the meat, the vegetables, the salad but bread is king.'
Louis Bromfield, American author (1896–1956)

For too long, we have been victims of tasteless, anonymous, identically shaped, characterless, boring bread... Sliced and bagged, clone-like, forming an orderly queue on the shelves waiting to be taken home to bloat out and carb up another unsuspecting individual.

Of course, it wasn't always like this.

No other foodstuff is more deeply rooted in history and civilisation than bread. In its most basic form – as flat bread made from crushed wheat – bread dates back some 30,000 years. The 'staff of life' was portioned to feed the poor, and spelt grain, which has been cultivated for over 7,000 years, is the wheat on which the Romans are said to have built their empire.

Some time ago (too long ago) the fires of the communal village ovens used to roar as village folk would sit and wait for the wild yeasts in their loaves to do their thing, for the crust to form and crackle and burst.

The communal ovens are long gone, but we can bring back real bread and make it accessible to everyone whatever your budget or lifestyle. We believe in bread that's lovingly crafted and shaped by hand, with each loaf having its own individual character. Bread that uses seasonal, locally sourced or foraged ingredients. Bread without additives, preservatives or flour treatment agents (all used by the large manufacturers wanting to make more bread, more quickly).

What we're talking about is the kind of bread that puts smiles on people's faces. This is one of the main reasons why we both gave up successful careers to start The Thoughtful Bread Company, an artisan bakery tucked away in the south-west of England. We started off small, working round the clock and thriftily scavenging everything (including the kitchen sink!) from restaurants undergoing refurbishments and bakeries up and down the country that had folded in the face of stiff competition from the supermarket giants.

Today, our award-winning bread is found in Michelin-starred restaurants, in the best delis and in children's lunchboxes. But we still make bread much as you would do at home. Or at least, you will do,

once we have taken you on this journey. Give your loaves the time they need to develop and we guarantee that when you get the knack, they will deliver in flavour and texture, again and again.

In the first part of the book, we'll guide you through bread-making essentials including kneading, proving and shaping. We'll also give you lots of thrifty tips about how to get kitted out with all the equipment your armoury will require. We'll show you how to use the money you've saved getting hold of your kit to source the very best ingredients your budget will allow.

In the next three sections, we'll talk you through bread recipes – both savoury and sweet – and show you how to make a meal out of them. This is the concept of bread as the king of the table – which simply means that if you've made the effort to bake some decent bread, then you're not far off from having a memorable meal to feed friends and family. Along the way we even divulge some tricks of the trade.

Finally we'll show you what to do with your leftovers. When that last slice of bread or unwanted crust is sat at those pearly white gates, we'll teach you how to turn it into the most heavenly of thrifty goodies. Crust to crust, we promise to reveal how every single morsel can be enjoyed – you'll have your bread-eating audience coming back for more again and again.

Bread-making is something we want you to take personally. The beauty of bread is that when made properly and in enough variety, there is something for all regardless of faith, personal taste or special dietary requirements. This book is for everyone – for parents on a budget wanting to send their children to school with something decent to eat in their packed lunch; for students who want to make a meal from the few bits and pieces that might be lying around in the fridge; and for anyone with people to entertain or food to knock up for an impromptu picnic or before the big match kicks off.

So rise up with us against the bagged and the boring, the bland and the tasteless! The Bread Revolution is here and we're waiting for you to join it.

**Duncan Glendinning and Patrick Ryan
of The Thoughtful Bread Company**

Bread – Real Bread, that is – needs only
four ingredients: flour, yeast, water and salt.
To begin your Bread Revolution, these cornerstone
ingredients are the ones to arm yourself with.

Patrick always says that you can't turn lead into
gold, and the end product will only ever be as good
as the ingredients you put into it. When we started
The Thoughtful Bread Company we decided to save
money on equipping the bakery so that we would
have the cash to buy the very best ingredients –
especially the flour. We'll show you how you can
do the same and get brilliant results.

THE FOUR INGREDIENTS OF REAL BREAD

Flour is the heart and soul of your bread, and great bread needs great flour. When we started we bought ours from a small watermill close to where the bakery was born in south-west England. Now the business has grown, it comes from nearby Shipton Mill in Gloucestershire, where they make an incredible range of flours.

FINDING GOOD BREAD FLOUR

The price difference between good-quality flour and the cheaper stuff is so small compared with the world of difference it will make to your bread, it really is worth paying out for. Good flour has everything to do with the protein content of the wheat. A higher protein content helps to develop more gluten during the kneading process, giving you a better-textured loaf.

Always use strong bread flour, rather than plain (all-purpose) flour, which is more suited to cakes and pastry.

The wheat grain has three parts: the endosperm (where most of the starch is), the germ (with most of the protein) and the outer husk. If possible, buy flour labelled as stoneground. Other flours will most likely have been roller-milled. This is a more commercial way to produce flour, but it puts the grain through more pressure, which can affect the finished product.

We would normally recommend that you source locally, but depending on where you live this may not give the best results. The British weather, for example, is not conducive to good yields of hard wheat (the type with most protein), so in the UK it is best to opt for flours made from a combination of British and imported wheat.

YEAST

In most breads yeast is what helps the dough rise, or leaven. Yeast is a living organism that converts the natural sugars in the flour into (among other things) carbon dioxide. This is what creates all the little bubbles in your dough as it rises. The challenge for the baker is to use just enough yeast to get the job done — use too much and this will impair the flavour.

Yeast comes in three main forms: fresh, dried and fast-action. Fresh yeast, which is what we use, will give you the best flavour. It can be sourced from most bakeries or from the bakery counters of supermarkets that make their own bread, but has a short shelf life — keep it wrapped up and sealed in an airtight container in the fridge for a maximum of two weeks.

Active dried yeast and fast-action yeast can be found in the bakery aisles of supermarkets and many local stores. They can be stored in the cupboard and keep for longer than fresh yeast, but do have a stronger flavour and fast-action yeast tends to include additives. All yeast absorbs moisture once the packet is opened and loses its strength over time. Dried and fast-action yeast are more concentrated than fresh, so you use less.

TYPES OF FLOUR

Each type of flour, from each mill, has its own character. Some types absorb more water than others. You may find that your recipe requires a little more or a little less water — after all, this is what makes baking bread personal.

Strong white bread flour

This is produced by sifting wholemeal (whole-wheat) flour to remove some of the bran and germ to make a lighter flour. Buy unbleached where possible, and expect an off-white colour and lovely scent. This is a staple flour for everyday bread-making.

Fine-ground strong wholemeal (whole-wheat) flour

The coarseness or fineness of wholemeal flour depends on the amount of bran that has been sifted out after grinding. Most wholemeal flours that are easily available are fine ground.

Coarse strong wholemeal (whole-wheat) flour

We use this for our Irish soda bread (see page 76), which is all about the hearty texture that a coarsely ground flour gives you. It is not as easy to get hold of on the high street, but you can order it online (see page 168) or buy direct if you have a local mill.

Spelt flour

An ancient ancestor of modern wheat varieties, spelt is not wheat-free but is growing in popularity. As a more primitive grain with a simpler structure it is easier to break down and therefore more easily digestible if you have a wheat allergy or intolerance. You can find both wholemeal and white spelt flour.

Rye flour

Another good flour if you have a wheat allergy or intolerance. The downside is that it is low in gluten, so rye breads are denser and have a slightly gummier texture. Rye is often mixed with wheat for a lighter-textured bread that still has rye's distinctive flavour.

Rice flour

Ideal for gluten-free diets and stocked in supermarkets and wholefood shops, rice flour is used for the crust of our tasty tiger bread (see page 37). It can't be used on its own for bread and is usually combined with other gluten-free flours.

WATER

This activates the yeast and protein in the flour and brings the dough together. There is no need to use filtered or bottled water unless you live in an area where the water is heavily treated. We get ours from a borehole on the farm where our bakery is based, but when we make bread at home or at friends' houses we use water straight from the tap.

You may also read about the temperature of the water being vital in bread-making, but as long as it is lukewarm or room temperature or you will be fine. The main thing to avoid is using hot water, as this will kill off the yeast.

We have given the amount of water in millilitres, but if you want to be really accurate you could use digital scales to weigh it rather than relying on a measuring jug. You simply use the same weight in grams as the volume we have given in millilitres — 100 ml of water converts to 100 g. This rule of thumb also works for milk, but is not exact for heavier liquids such as oil.

SALT

A natural flavour enhancer, salt has been used for thousands of years as a way of preserving food. It was also a currency in Roman times, giving rise to the saying 'a man worth his salt'.

Salt has had a lot of bad press for its negative health effects, but the amount used in home-made bread is modest compared with the quantities in processed foods, and in bread-making, salt is an essential ingredient. It regulates the yeast activity in your dough and helps the flour to absorb water — try making a dough without salt and see how sticky it gets.

Choose natural sea salt over the cheaper processed kinds, which often contain additives such as anti-caking agents. Fine sea salt will dissolve more easily.

While salt is essential, avoid direct contact between yeast and salt at all costs as they are not good friends. Salt in concentration will kill off the yeast so is best blended with the flour beforehand.

WATER

SALT

YEAST

FLOUR ↓

ALSO IN YOUR REAL BREAD SUPPLIES...

EGGS

We are lucky enough to have a beautiful brood of hens at the bakery who lay the most delicious eggs (and get their fair share of tasty seed in return). If you have ever tried freshly laid eggs from genuinely free-range chickens you will know that the difference is startling — not only the taste, but the colour of the yolk. It is beautifully golden, compared with the pale, colourless appearance of their mass-produced counterparts.

A good egg makes all the difference in baking (see the brioche recipe on page 124), so if you have a local farm or know someone who keeps chickens in their garden why not offer them a barter — bread in return for delicious fresh eggs.

Or try keeping your own hens. You need only a relatively small amount of space and the upkeep is not labour-intensive or time-consuming. Ex-battery hens are often available for a very small cost, and giving them a new home is so rewarding.

BUTTER & MILK

Butter and milk both help to develop a rich flavour in bread. Butter (and other fats such as rapeseed oil or olive oil) will also give the bread slightly better keeping qualities and a softer texture.

We buy from our local depot as we need rather large quantities. We do, however, always read the labels to make sure that the milk is locally produced. It's a way to support our dairy farmers.

SUGAR

Think of sugar as food for yeast. Flour contains natural sugars so adding more sugar isn't absolutely necessary, but it helps the bread to prove up and also contributes to the flavour. For the recipes in this book opt for unrefined sugars — golden caster (superfine), soft or dark brown sugar, demerara or even molasses — over processed white sugars, as they will be more easily digested by the yeast.

When we do want white sugar we use one made from sugar beets here in Britain so we can cut down on food miles. For demerara and other unrefined sugars made from sugar cane look for those marked as Fairtrade.

FORAGING & NEARLY FREE

The very best ingredients don't have to cost the world. While we believe it is worth investing in good flour, cheese and eggs, the wild larder has an abundance of produce that is ripe for the picking, and free! At The Thoughtful Bread Company we always try to have at least one bread on sale that champions food from the wild larder.

Here is a handful of foraged ingredients that we use in a number of the recipes in this book and provide a great introduction to food for free. They are common through most of the UK, but take a good local foraging guidebook and discover what you have close to home.

WILD GARLIC (RAMSONS)

In spring you'll smell the pungent, fresh, garlicky aroma as you approach wooded areas. Our favourite ingredient from the wild larder, wild garlic tends to grow in large patches. Free food doesn't get better than this. The leaves are great in salads, sautéed and added to flavour a bread, or used in pesto (see page 91).

NETTLES

These are available year round but are best picked in the spring from overgrown gardens, hedgerows, woods and riverbanks. Wearing gloves, pinch off the top two sets of leaves from plants that haven't yet gone to seed. Blanch them as you would spinach (to remove the sting!). We season ours with grated nutmeg and it makes the fragrant nettle & chive bread on page 46, packed full of vitamin C and iron.

CHICKWEED

Available all year in back gardens, wastelands and hedgerows, chickweed produces tender shoots with a pleasant, pea-like flavour that are great raw in salads. We put them in the panzanella salad (see page 144).

JACK-BY-THE-HEDGE

Found in back gardens, woods and along footpaths in early spring, the young leaves add a mild garlicky and mustardy flavour to salads.

HAZELNUTS, COBNUTS & WALNUTS

Hazelnuts and cobnuts (a type of hazel) are abundant along footpaths and in woods. They ripen and drop from the trees from early autumn. Walnuts are less common but if you have any trees nearby, then make the most of them. Pick the walnuts as the bitter, fleshy outer skin dries and splits open to reveal the hard-cased nut. Use in breads (see page 60) and dips (page 91), or in salads (page 63).

BLACKBERRIES

These are available from late summer – not just in the autumn – everywhere from woods and hedges to back gardens. The lowest-hanging berries in a cluster are usually the ripest. Once washed they freeze well and make fantastic jam or compote (see page 154).

GROW YOUR OWN HERBS

Aside from what the wild larder has to offer, you can have a go at growing your own herbs, veg or even fruit with very little space. A balcony or even a windowsill will do just fine, but with a small patio garden or a neglected flowerbed the possibilities are endless!

At Thoughtful HQ, we got tired of buying fresh herbs that can easily be grown in the UK, only to find out they were being raised thousands of miles away, or in conflict-ridden, water-starved countries where the growers need their water to raise enough food for themselves. So we bought some young plants from a nearby nursery for the price of a few packs of cut herbs and made our own herb bed.

A year on, you can't see the soil for the sheer amount of foliage and we are virtually self-sufficient for all our herb needs.

OUR TOP RECOMMENDATIONS FOR GROWING YOUR OWN

Sage

The perfect partner for pork or fish, sage is easy to grow from a small starter plant. Protect with a fleece in the coldest winters, and keep picking the young leaves through the summer to encourage more foliage. Dry or freeze any excess, or use to infuse oils.

Thyme

Deliciously fragrant, thyme is a real all-rounder. We plumped for the creeping and carpeting varieties as they will slowly spread to provide attractive ground cover that acts as a natural weed suppressant.

Rosemary

If you know someone with a bush the best way to grow rosemary is from young shoots, around 10 cm (4 in) long. Dip them into rooting compound, plant them up and, fingers crossed, they will take. Rosemary makes the perfect combo with garlic to infuse olive oil for dipping or enriching your focaccias (see page 100).

Chives

Unlike the other herbs here, chives are easy to grow from seed, and a really versatile way to introduce that mild onion flavour to breads.

VEG THAT ARE WORTH HAVING A STAB AT TOO...

Tomatoes

You can easily grow tomatoes from seed, or it is pretty cheap to pick up young plants from the garden centre. If you're clever with the space and the varieties you choose you can really land yourself a bountiful crop.

A growbag on the patio works well, while some great varieties of cherry or tumbling tomatoes can be grown in hanging baskets or big plant pots. Treat them to a tomato feed (make your own by soaking nettles in water for a week) when they start to flower, and keep well watered. There is nothing like picking a fresh tomato straight off the plant and popping it in your mouth!

Chillies

These may sound exotic but they are actually quite simple to raise at home. We are lucky enough to have a polythene-covered geodome where we can grow rather a lot of chillies, but even just the one plant will give you a decent yield. From the Scorpions to the Habaneros, the Rings of Fire to the Apaches, the names are great fun and the plants themselves are beautifully ornamental when in flower. Chillies make a really rather tasty addition to breads, butters, oil infusions (see page 114) and more. If you have extra, consider drying or freezing.

TIPS FOR THOUGHTFUL FORAGING

→ Always pack a light bag when you are off on walks — you never know what gems you might uncover!

→ Don't pick unless you have definitely identified the species to avoid potentially poisonous varieties — especially with fungi.

→ Ask for the landowner's permission before you start picking.

→ Avoid roadsides or any fields where chemicals may be sprayed.

→ Don't pick your whole hoard from the same patch — spread out so you leave some for others.

URBAN FORAGING

Some people use this term to mean making the most of what the wild larder has to offer in and around our cities. At The Thoughtful Bread Company we have an altogether different meaning for 'urban foraging'. When we are short on herbs, or whenever we spot a laden tree with fruits dropping, we love to knock on people's doors and, with all our smiles and as much charm as we can muster, ask whether we can help ourselves. We suggest you do the same!

We have never, to date, had anything other than a warm welcome. You'll be surprised how many people have a huge rosemary bush in their front garden and are unaware of its existence or culinary capabilities, or are happy to find someone willing to unburden them of the spoils of their fruit trees — no one likes to see it going to waste. Why not offer them a fresh loaf next time you are passing through?

HORSERADISH

WILD PLUMS

MMM!

SWEET

TOOLS OF THE TRADE

When you start baking there's some essential kit that you'll need. The good news is that you probably already have a lot you can use in kitchen cupboards.

1 Baking tins

We are proud that not a single tin of ours was bought new, and some must be 50 years old. Speak to friends, family or colleagues and ask if they have an 'orphan' tin stashed away that you can adopt — you could thank them with home-made bread. The two you really want to get hold of are 400 g and 800 g tins, or their imperial counterparts, 1 lb and 2 lb tins. You can also make free-form loaves that cook on a baking tray.

2 Proving bowls

These hold the shape of a free-form loaf while it is proving. The ideal sizes are 1 litre (1¾ pints) for 400 g loaves and 2 litre (3½ pints) for 800 g loaves. Many artisan bakeries use 'banneton' or 'brotform' bowls made from cane, which give a ribbed appearance, but you can use any plastic, glass or ceramic bowl.

3 Couche cloths

'Couche' means 'layer' and these act as a layer between your bread and your proving bowl. Without them you run the risk of all your hard work getting stuck. Bakery suppliers sell hemmed cloths or fabric by the metre, but you can use any natural, unbleached and untreated fibre. We found that dust sheets from DIY shops are ideal — although bakery suppliers would probably rather you didn't know that!

4 Baking stone

This will help your free-form loaves produce a good crust. You can pick them up in most kitchen and home stores and on the internet. Or else turn up at your local stone mason with a big smiley face and ask for an off-cut of marble or granite 2 cm (1 in) thick.

5 Digital scales

This is one bit of kit we suggest you invest decent money in. Getting your quantities right is crucial in bread-making. Ensure your scales will weigh as little as 1 g and as much as 2-3 kg. Opt for ones with a power adapter or rechargeable batteries.

6 Dough scraper

While this isn't an essential tool it is a huge time-saver. Dough scrapers normally come with one rounded edge for cutting the dough into portions, and a straight edge for scraping down your worktop and bringing a wet dough together.

7 Lame

Pronounced 'lam' and also called a 'grignette', this baker's blade is invaluable for scoring your loaves. The type with a separate blade handle that takes double-edged razor blades means you can simply change the blade when it is blunt. If necessary, you can get away with a serrated knife or a very, very sharp knife.

8 Timer

There is nothing worse than putting all your heart into a beautiful loaf only to be distracted and pick up the smell of burnt bread. It has happened to us more than once. Or use your mobile phone's timer function.

OTHER KIT

Rolling pin

A good, sturdy, wooden rolling pin is what you need for things like the crispy bacon fougasse sticks (see page 108). Duncan has improvised with an empty wine bottle on a few occasions.

Measuring jugs

Great for holding and mixing your liquids.

Oven mitts

While burns on our arms are our bakers' war-wounds, they are best avoided if you can.

Cooling rack

Needed because hot bread left on a flat surface will invariably start to sweat, which can soften the crust.

Spray bottle

Easily found in garden centres and a handy tool to mist the oven with, or spray loaves before garnishing.

Plus…

A flour shaker or fine sieve; an apron (baking is a messy job); clean tea towels (dish towels).

JOHN COMPTON

PAUL TRINDER

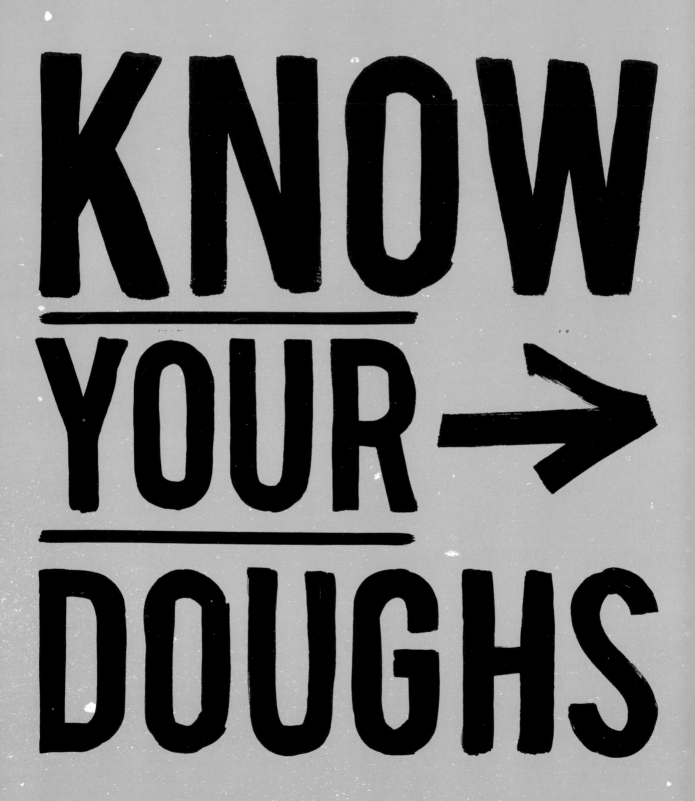

Welcome to the Bread Revolution. This section is where we hope to lay the foundations from which your bread-making skills will grow. Many of the recipes in this book are based on the techniques explained here. So if you have ever wondered what the windowpane effect is or what knocking back involves, this is the place to find it. And if you've never heard of either, don't worry.

There's no better way to learn baking than by doing it, so we've explained the key stages of working with dough by taking you through making a loaf.

Over the page we've given the recipe for an everyday white bread that you can then adapt to a wholemeal loaf, different shapes such as rolls, plaits and rustic breads, and variations such as tiger bread and a spelt honey loaf. These basics are quick to master, and it won't be long before you realise how versatile and creative dough can be. With these baking secrets you'll soon be knocking out beautiful loaves of your own.

MAKE THIS BOOK YOUR OWN

Feel free to write all over the recipes in this book, as we've shown on the white bread here. All flours are different, and may need more or less water, while for loaves such as the local cheese loaf (see page 54), you may want a bit less cheese if it is especially strong. Keep this book in the kitchen, adapt the recipes to work for you and make it your own!

EVERYDAY WHITE BREAD

This is your basic loaf, the one for the kids' sandwiches and smothering with butter and jam. It's also great for learning the stages of bread-making, so refer back to the instructions here when you want a refresher while making the other recipes in this book.

Makes 2 small (400 g or 1 lb) loaves or 1 large (800 g or 2 lb) loaf

310 ml for my favourite flour

500 g (1 lb 2 oz / 3 ⅓ cups) strong white bread flour

10 g (2 tsp) fine sea salt

15 g (3 tsp) fresh yeast or 10 g (2 tsp) dried or fast-action yeast

300 ml (10 ½ fl oz) water

5 tsp rapeseed or olive oil

2 x 400 g (or 1 lb) loaf tins or 1 x 800 g (or 2 lb) tin

a little flour for dusting, or egg wash (see page 36)

a handful of ice cubes, or cold water, for steaming the oven

❶ MIXING TOGETHER THE DRY INGREDIENTS

First combine the flour and salt. You can do this either in a bowl or on a clean kitchen surface. Then make a well in the centre.

Mixing is as important a stage as any other. When you mix in an ingredient think about its purpose. Have you ever made a loaf that tasted bland, or refused to rise? This can be down to the mixing stage. Salt is essential in bread-making, but put it in direct contact with the yeast and the yeast will die. So always mix the salt through the flour first. If a recipe calls for sugar this is also often added to the flour now too. For purists,

bread is considered 'real' only when it is made solely by hand. We're not that hardline about it, but we do recommend that you get your hands dirty at least once – you will develop a better understanding and feel for the dough, and it's also very therapeutic.

We'll be assuming that hand-mixing is your tool of choice, as not everyone has a mixer. But if you do, then attach that dough hook (note that mixing times will generally be slightly less).

❷ ADDING YEAST & LIQUIDS

Crumble up the yeast and add it to the water, stirring it in so that it dissolves. If you don't have access to fresh yeast we have also given the amount of dried or fast-action yeast to use. Note that with fast-action yeast, you add it to the flour, not the water.

Lukewarm water is best. You don't want it too hot, as that will kill the yeast; or too cold, because that will slow down its activity. Blood temperature is ideal. Think of your yeast like a baby you're giving a bottle to: you want the water just nice and tepid.

Pour the yeasted water into the well along with the oil. If a recipe calls for oil or melted butter, don't pour it directly on to the yeast as the fat molecules will coat it, inhibiting its activity.

Next start incorporating the flour. You can use your hands, a spatula or a fork. The dough will begin to come together into a ball. At this point turn it out on to a clean kitchen surface. Stainless steel or something cold and smooth, such as granite or marble, is ideal, but a kitchen worktop is fine too.

❸ KNEADING

This is when we draw out the magic in the flour. When flour absorbs water the proteins in it form bonds to make elastic chains of gluten. Kneading gives the gluten a good workout, stretching it so that it becomes stronger and more flexible. Everyone has their own technique, but you do need to get your hands really stuck in and keep at it for about 10 minutes. The way Patrick kneads is to push the dough away with the heel of one hand, then fold it back over towards him, and give it a nifty quarter turn before stretching it again.

If the dough feels a little tight and firm you can add a little more water. Make a well in the centre of your ball of dough and sprinkle in a tablespoon or two of water, then work it in fully by kneading.

④ CHECKING THE STRETCH

When you knead by hand you can feel the dough change in texture. When ready, it will become much smoother and more elastic, and stretch without tearing. It should no longer be sticky.

Keep faith with the dough as you knead. It may stick to your work surface at first, but resist the temptation to add more flour. If you find the dough sticking to your hands, wet them with a little oil or water.

As you continue kneading you'll notice the dough pulling away more easily from the surface. A dough scraper (see page 20) is great for gathering it back together into a ball when it does stick.

In our recipes we suggest that you check for the windowpane effect (see opposite), rather than simply following the time. This is the surest test of when the dough is ready and has had enough kneading.

⑤ PROVING

Place the ball of dough in a lightly oiled bowl and cover the bowl with a damp cloth or oiled clingfilm. Leave in a fairly warm – but not hot – place for 60–90 minutes or until the ball has doubled in size.

For the proving times in this book we have assumed a temperature of about 20°C (70°F). But as conditions vary, the times are just a guide. The best thing is to keep an eye on how much your dough has risen.

This is the stage where we can turn average bread into great bread. During proving, the yeast converts sugars and starch from the flour into carbon dioxide and alcohol. The gas makes the dough rise and the whole process enhances the flavour.

The challenge is striking the right balance between allowing enough fermentation to maximise taste, and not letting it go too far. If the dough is left to prove for too long, or if it gets too warm, the structure suffers and the loaf may have an alcoholic aftertaste.

⑥ KNOCKING BACK

Once your dough has reached the optimum stage of proving, it's essential to stop it in its tracks so that it doesn't over-prove. Simply turn the dough out on to a clean kitchen surface and punch it down, then fold the outside edges into the middle.

Knocking back releases the gas that has built up during proving, equalises the temperature inside and outside the dough, and begins a new cycle.

Once you have knocked it back, turn the dough ball up the other way, so that the tucked side is underneath. Now it is ready for shaping.

⑦ SHAPING

First you will need to portion the dough into the size of loaf – or rolls – that you want. Most of our recipes will give you two small loaves or one large loaf. This white bread recipe is also enough for 12 dinner rolls. If you really want to make sure your loaves or rolls are equal, weigh out the portions of dough.

A dough scraper is ideal for cutting, but you could also use a sharp knife. Try to avoid cutting lots of small pieces then pushing them together. The loaf will benefit from not being made up from several smaller amounts.

Shaping the dough is where you really get to express yourself. A freshly baked loaf straight from a tin – as we'll show you below – can be amazing, but there are plenty of other options, each with their own personality. The plainest of doughs can be transformed by shaping. For instructions on free-form loaves (baked on a tray or pizza stone) and rolls see page 40.

⑧ FORMING A TIN LOAF

To form a tin loaf, make sure the dough is smooth side up on a clean kitchen surface. Resist the temptation to cover the surface in flour – you will almost always be able to shape it without.

Flatten the dough into a rectangle – you can do this by holding the two sides and pulling and shaking the dough up and down a little to lengthen it – then take the two ends and bring them to the centre so that they meet. Push down with your knuckles to seal. Fold the top and bottom of the dough in towards the middle, as if you were forming an envelope. Flip the loaf so that the seam is underneath and roll it slightly with your hands to mould the dough together. Lightly oil the loaf tin and place the shaped dough in the bottom.

CONTINUES ON PAGE 32 >

MIXING

KNEADING

PROVING

KNOCKING BACK

SHAPING

THE WINDOWPANE EFFECT

THE WINDOWPANE EFFECT

What you are looking to achieve with kneading is what's known as the windowpane effect. When you stretch the dough thinly, it should be able to stretch so much that you can see light through it. If you find your dough is tearing easily, it's telling you it needs a couple more minutes' kneading. By kneading well, your bread will rise better and have a soft, even texture.

SCISSOR-CUTTING

SPRINGY

TURTLE

❾ SECOND PROVING

Once you have shaped your dough leave it prove for a second and final time. For rolls and free-form loaves, place them on a lightly oiled baking tray. It is important to keep the dough covered to prevent a skin forming. Lightly oiled clingfilm works well, but don't cover too tightly – allow room for the dough to grow. Alternatively, spray the dough surface with oil, smooth over lightly and cover with a damp cloth.

Prove the dough for about 60 minutes or until it has risen to the crest of the tin or by about two-thirds of its original size. (If the bread is proved to fully double its size there is a danger it will have over-proved and the loaf will collapse.) The dough should be firm but spring back when you press it with your finger.

❿ PREHEATING THE OVEN

Oven temperature will vary depending on the recipe, but in general we start by preheating the oven to 230°C (450°F/Gas 8), then adjusting. Place a roasting tray in the bottom – we will use this when the bread goes in.

⓫ GARNISHING & SCORING

Many breads call for a final garnish. For a classic split tin either dust your loaf with flour or give it a golden finish with an egg glaze (see page 36).

Scoring involves cutting the surface of the dough, either with a single line (for a split tin loaf) or a pattern of cuts. Back when communal ovens were commonplace, scoring unique patterns on the bread helped to distinguish your loaves from your neighbours'. We talk of giving the loaf its 'signature' for this reason. Scoring gives your loaf individuality and also allows gas to escape that might otherwise burst through any weak areas.

The ideal implement for scoring is a razor blade in a special handle, known as a lame (see page 20), but you could use a sharp serrated knife. Be confident and use quick, single motions. Try not to cut downwards, as the blade will work its way through the dough. A little leftover dough is good to practise on.

⓬ BAKING

The secret to achieving a great crust and beautifully risen loaf is steam. The steam helps to protect the loaves from the intense heat, so the dough can continue to rise and burst open before the crust sets. Most professional ovens release a blast of steam when the loaves have been put in. A simple way to achieve this at home is to place a roasting tray in the oven as it preheats, then drop in a handful of ice cubes or a splash of cold water when you put your loaf in to bake. Close the oven door immediately to trap the steam. Alternatively, use a spray bottle to mist the oven as the loaves are put in. You can mist the oven walls several times in the first 10 minutes of baking.

⓭ SETTING THE COOKING TIME

Most recipes call for a cooking time of approximately 35–40 minutes, but this will depend on the recipe. When baking a loaf really try to push the baking time as far as possible, as it will give you a better crust.

For this white bread, place the tins or baking tray in the preheated oven and add the ice cubes to the roasting tray. Set your timer and after 10 minutes reduce the oven temperature to 210°C (425°F/Gas 6–7), remove the roasting tray and continue baking for another 15 minutes.

Remove the loaves from the tins and return them to the oven for a further 10 minutes. You may find you need to rotate the loaves to ensure even cooking.

⓮ CHECKING & COOLING

The simplest way to check that your loaf is cooked is to tap gently on the base. If you hear a hollow sound it is done.

Tip out the loaf from the tin, running a knife around the edge if necessary, and place it on a wire rack to cool. Try to resist the temptation to tuck in before the bread has cooled – but if your best intentions fail, then simply eat, share and enjoy!

⓯ STORING YOUR BREAD

Crusty bread is best stored in paper. Don't wrap it in plastic unless you plan to freeze it, as the loaf will soften. On the other hand, soft bread, like a sandwich loaf, is best stored wrapped in plastic or frozen. If freezing, pre-slice the loaf so that you need only take out what you need. All bread should be stored in a dark, cool place – but not in the fridge.

To defrost a frozen loaf in the oven, wrap the bread in a clean cloth that has been soaked in warm water and then wrung out. Place in a warm oven at 100°C (200°F/Gas ½) for 20–25 minutes, re-wetting the cloth as needed. To bring back the crust remove the cloth and turn up the oven to 220°C (425°F/Gas 7) for 5–10 minutes.

FITTING BREAD-MAKING AROUND YOUR SCHEDULE

The average proving time of a loaf conveniently happens to fit itself around the length of a rugby match or film. Your dough could be kneaded before you sit down for the pre-match build-up, left to prove for 60–90 minutes, knocked back and shaped during half-time and put in the oven to bake an hour later, during the post-match interviews. It is almost as if they were intended to go hand in hand.

We believe bread-making can easily be made to work round your day. Begin the whole process about four hours before you want to eat your loaves.

Weekend lunch loaves

Start making your dough once you're up and about at the weekend – a quick bit of kneading and you're on your way. It will have proved after 60–90 minutes – time for the gym or shops. With a quick bit of shaping, get the loaf on to prove about an hour and 40 minutes before you plan to eat, and you'll have it in time for lunch.

Breakfast bread

Certain doughs can be made the night before. Knead, prove and shape your dough then leave it to rise in the fridge overnight. With all the hard work done all that is left to do is bake. This works well for the cinnamon swirls (page 126) and Bath buns (page 129).

NOT THE PERFECT LOAF?

Dough won't rise

The yeast may be past its sell-by date. If you find that the dough simply isn't moving it can be saved by dissolving some new yeast in a minimal amount of water and working it into the dough just enough to ensure that it is evenly distributed.

Bread is soft and pale

The bread may not have been baked for long enough, or the oven temperature was too low. A fully cooked loaf should sound hollow when tapped on the base.

Crust is too soft

This can happen if you don't have enough steam in the oven (see page 32). Try to avoid banging that oven door, as this creates a draught.

Loaf is crumbly and dry

You may have cooked the loaf for too long or used too much flour. The ideal dough is supple like a welcoming pillow. If the dough feels dry you can add a little extra liquid (see page 28).

Loaf collapses in the oven

Most likely you left the dough for too long during the second prove and it has over-risen (see page 32).

Loaf is dense and flat

If you do not knead the dough enough it will be unable to rise and expand without tearing and collapsing, resulting in a dense heavy loaf. The dough will always tell you when it has had enough – look for the windowpane effect (see page 29). Alternatively, if you added too much liquid the dough will not be strong enough to support itself as it proves. Don't prove your dough in too warm a place as this may kill the yeast.

Bread has a yeasty flavour

You used too much yeast. Don't add extra yeast to make the dough rise faster, just wait a little longer. With bread, patience is a virtue – it will rise in the end.

Large holes in the dough

If you have large holes or what appears like a tunnel running through the dough, it wasn't knocked back properly. Take your time when shaping your dough.

Bread tastes bland

You didn't use enough salt (see page 13).

Crust cracks after cooling

The oven was too hot and you left the bread in a draught when it was cooling.

Loaf has a flat top

You need to ensure that you use a good-quality flour (see page 12). You may have used too little salt or the dough could be too wet.

Crust splits on one side of the loaf

It was too close to the oven wall during baking. As every oven differs you may need to turn your bread during baking to ensure even cooking.

GARNISHES & GLAZES

GARNISHES TO TOP YOUR LOAF

Garnishing a loaf is like getting ready for a big night out – throwing on your best shirt or fixing your make-up. It helps to give your bread that finishing touch.

Whether a sprinkling of sesame or poppy seeds, rolled oats or fresh herbs, these toppings alter the appearance, flavour and texture of the bread. They are also a way to make your loaf stand out from the crowd. When choosing which to use, the rules are simple: make sure the garnish is appropriate, edible, and that it complements the finished bread. Add the toppings just before baking – give the loaf a spray of water first to help the garnish stick.

Flour – a sprinkle of white, wholemeal or granary flour gives a more rustic, farmhouse look, or use bran on a wholemeal (whole-wheat) loaf.

Seeds – sesame, poppy and linseeds all work well, adding flavour and crunch.

Sea salt – a spray of water and a light sprinkle adds a crunchy finish that's especially effective on bagels.

Rolled oats – these decorate a multi-grain loaf and look great spread across bread rolls and baps.

Cracked black pepper, chilli or paprika – along with a drizzle of oil, these deliver a touch of colour and spice. Try them on focaccia (see page 100).

Nuts – almonds, hazelnuts or walnuts are great on sweet breads, giving a little taste of what is inside.

Fresh herbs – sprinkle herbs on to loaves or press them into focaccia either before baking or just after.

Sugar – a brush of milk and a sprinkle of brown sugar gives your finished bread a lovely crunch.

GLAZES TO MAKE IT SHINE

Applied before baking these introduce moisture, helping to change the consistency and flavour of the crust. You can also use them as a great adhesive to help any garnish stick. Glazes added after baking give flavour and a glossy finish.

BEFORE BAKING
These glazes are commonly used on savoury breads.

Milk – gives a softer, golden crust.

Olive oil – adds flavour and a shiny finish.

Butter – a brush of melted butter adds a rich flavour and colour.

Salt water – mist with a solution of 1 tsp of sea salt dissolved in 50 ml of water for a crisp crust.

Egg white – mixed with a drop of water this gives a lightly golden, shiny crust.

Egg wash – for the best egg wash mix 1 egg yolk with 1 whole egg and a pinch of salt. It produces a rich, golden finish that almost sparkles.

AFTER BAKING
For a soft, shiny, almost sticky finish, brush on the glaze after baking. These are most often used on sweet breads and pastries.

Butter – brush on melted butter to soften the crust.

Honey – warm gently and brush on.

Sugar glaze – bring 50 g (1¾ oz / ¼ cup) sugar and 50 ml water to the boil in a pan, stirring until the sugar has dissolved. Boil for five minutes, until reduced to a syrup, then brush over the loaf for a glossy sheen.

Lemon syrup – use the sugar glaze recipe above, but boil until reduced by about a third and then add the juice of 2 lemons. Drizzle over to add citrus flavour.

Icing sugar glaze – 30 g (1 oz / ¼ cup) icing (confectioners') sugar mixed with 3 tsp of milk or cream forms a lovely icing that can be drizzled over a sweet bread once cooled.

Jams and preserves – warm gently and thin with a little water or liqueur. Apricot jam is a great all-rounder.

TIGER BREAD

The secret of tiger bread is the rice flour glaze. The characteristic stripes are formed by brushing a paste over the loaf before you bake it. As the bread expands the glaze cracks and bakes to a rusty gold. The bread beneath is the basic white loaf recipe on page 27.

Makes 2 small 400 g or 1 lb loaves

800 g (2 lb) white bread dough (see page 27)

For the paste:

180 g (6 ½ oz) rice flour

60 g (2 ¼ oz) plain white (all-purpose) flour

10 g (2 tsp) fine sea salt

24 g (5 tsp) golden caster (superfine) sugar

200 ml (7 fl oz) water

24 g (5 tsp) fresh yeast or 14 g (3 tsp) dried or fast-action yeast

♠ Follow the instructions for making the white bread, then while it is proving for the first time make the tiger bread paste. Mix together the flours, salt and sugar in a bowl, add the water and crumble in the yeast. Continue mixing until you have the consistency of wallpaper paste.

♠ Knock back the dough and divide it into two. Line a baking tray with baking parchment, then shape each piece of dough into a ball (see page 40) and place it seam-side down on the tray. Paint the whole of each loaf thickly with the paste and leave to prove for about 40 minutes.

♠ Preheat the oven to 230°C (450°F/Gas 8) and bake as for the everyday white loaf, reducing the temperature to 200°C (400°F/Gas 6) after 15 minutes. Continue baking for a further 20 minutes until the glaze is a rich golden brown and the base of the loaf sounds hollow when tapped.

HEARTY WHOLEMEAL

Wholemeal flour generally requires a little more care than white, and can need greater encouragement to rise. But it more than makes up for this in depth of flavour – and it is the full nutritional package. For this recipe we use a coarse wholemeal flour, as it gives fantastic texture and taste.

Makes 2 small 400 g or 1 lb loaves

500 g (1 lb 2 oz / 3⅓ cups) coarse strong wholemeal (whole-wheat) flour

10 g (2 tsp) dark brown sugar

10 g (2 tsp) fine sea salt

15 g (3 tsp) fresh yeast or 10 g (2 tsp) dried or fast-action yeast

330 ml (11¼ fl oz / 1⅓ cups) water

3 tsp honey

25 g (5 tsp) rapeseed or olive oil

Makes 2 small 400 g or 1 lb loaves

500 g (1 lb 2 oz / 3⅓ cups) wholemeal spelt flour

15 g (3 tsp) fine sea salt

10 g (2 tsp) fresh yeast or 7 g (1½ tsp) dried or fast-action yeast

300 ml (10½ fl oz) water

3 tsp honey

♠ Combine the flour, sugar and salt in a bowl and make a well in the centre. Crumble the yeast into the water and stir to dissolve. Add the yeasted water to the well, along with the honey and oil, and bring together into a dough with your hands or with a spatula. Turn the dough out on to a clean kitchen surface and knead for 10 minutes or until you achieve the windowpane effect (see page 29). If you find the dough a little wet don't panic, as wholemeal flour tends to absorb water more slowly than white. Resist the temptation to add more flour, as it will come together.

♠ Place the dough in a lightly oiled bowl, cover with a damp cloth and leave to prove for 60-80 minutes or until doubled in size.

♠ Turn the proved dough out on to a clean work surface and knock it back. Divide the dough into two equal portions. Shape as for the white tin loaf (see page 27) and place into two lightly oiled 400g (1 lb) loaf tins, or make free-form loaves (see page 40). Cover with clingfilm or a damp cloth and leave to prove again for 60–90 minutes or until the dough has risen to the edge of the loaf tin or by two-thirds of its volume. Check on the dough's progress from time to time.

♠ Preheat the oven to 230°C (450°F/Gas 8) and put a roasting tray in the bottom. When the loaves have risen, dust the surface with wholemeal flour, then place in the oven and steam by adding ice cubes or cold water to the tray. After 10 minutes reduce the oven temperature to 210°C (410°F/Gas 6) and bake for a further 10 minutes. Remove from the tins and bake for a final 10-20 minutes. Place on a wire rack to cool.

HONEY SPELT LOAF

♠ There has been a lot of talk about spelt flour in recent times and it continues to grow in popularity, largely down to its perceived nutritional benefits and easier digestive qualities (see page 13). Spelt is a more primitive grain than its cousin, common wheat. If you ever see it growing in a field it will be towering high, often reaching over two metres (six feet). It is a fantastic grain to work with and has a wonderful flavour. Follow the same method as for the wholemeal loaves (above).

BREAD SHAPES

BALL-SHAPED FREE-FORM LOAVES

1 Cob or ball
Fold all the outside edges into the centre, turn over so the smooth side is on top, then circle the ball around on the kitchen surface between your hands to smooth the edges.

2 Coburg
A cob with a cross cut into the centre.

3 Cottage loaf
Make two balls, one a third the size of the other. Spray the surfaces that will touch with water and press the smaller ball on top. Push the handle of a wooden spoon up through the bottom of the loaf until it comes through the top, then pull it back down to seal the dough balls together.

4 Pouch
Take your dough ball and press down about a third of the way in from one side. Roll this part of the dough to about 1 cm (½ in) or so thick. Spray with water and fold the rolled flap over the top of the ball.

LONG FREE-FORM LOAVES

5 Bloomer
Flatten the dough and stretch it out to a rough rectangle then roll it up into a rough sausage shape. Turn over so the seam is underneath and cut diagonal slashes in the top.

6 Baguette
Shape like a bloomer then roll the dough out like a sausage with your hands, working from the inside out to lengthen it. Let the loaf rest for two minutes, then roll again until it is long enough.

7 Epi
Literally 'wheat ear'. Roll the dough into a baguette shape then give it a series of alternating scissor cuts.

8 Plait
Roll three even portions of dough into equal sausages. Lay them out and pinch the top ends together. To plait, lift each outer sausage into the centre, alternating sides. Pinch the bottom ends together.

TIN LOAVES

9 Plain tin
Form following the instructions on page 27.

10 Split tin
Slash along the centre.

ROLLS & VARIATIONS

11 Ball-shaped rolls or burger buns
Follow the method for the cob (1), using 100 g (3½ oz) of dough for a lunch-size roll. Circle the dough balls on your kitchen surface by cupping one hand over them.

12 Torpedo rolls
Use the same method as for the baguette, but with roll-sized pieces of dough and keeping them shorter. Roll the dough with your hands to make a sausage, folding in and rolling to reach the shape you want.

13 Scissor cut
Snip the top of the roll or loaf with scissors.

14 Knotted roll
Roll a long strip of dough and then tie it in a simple knot, making a loop and pushing the end through with your finger. You'll need a length of about 30 cm (12 in).

OTHER SHAPES

15 Tear and share
This is really a series of ball-shaped rolls. Form as many as you would like and arrange on a floured tray so they are all touching. As they prove they will merge together, but then be easy to tear off when cooked.

16 Clay pot bread
This bread really is baked in a clay flowerpot.

17 Fougasse
See page 109.

18 Spiral
Roll a long baguette, mist with water and form a spiral.

19 Couronne bordelaise
See page 121.

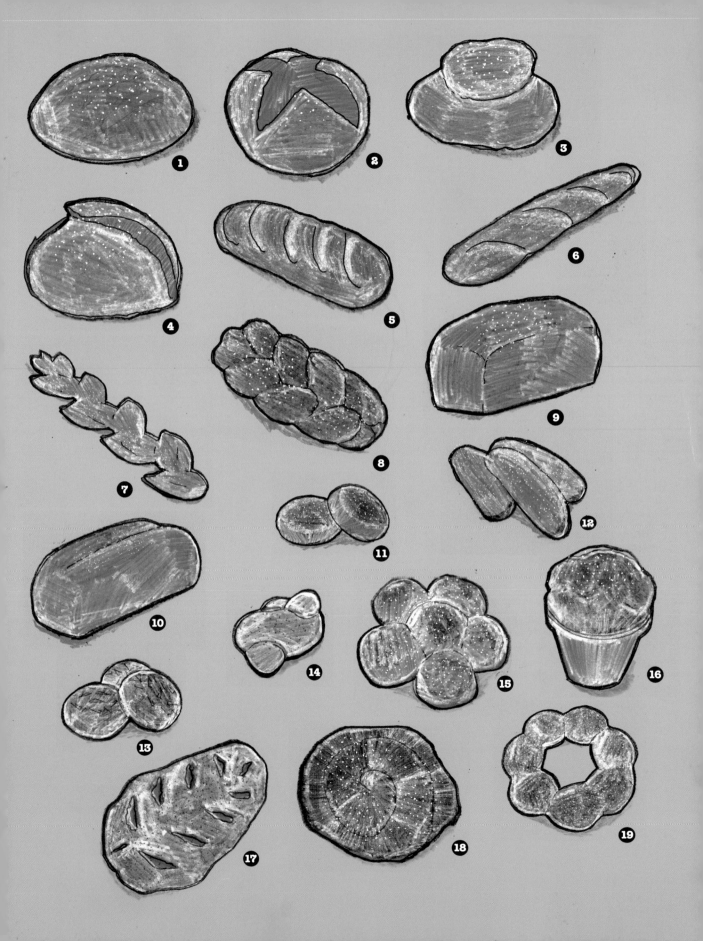

SAVOURY BREADS TO FEED THE TROOPS

Throughout this book our challenge is to help you experiment with your bread-making skills. The variety of forms that bread can take is endless, its versatility is unrivalled.

By using high-quality local, seasonal ingredients the results can only be fantastic. We'd like to introduce you to some of our favourite recipes, as well as breads that we're always being asked about at The Thoughtful Bread Company.

Once you've put all the care and effort into making your loaves, rolls or crackers, you can either just tuck in – perhaps with a spread of home-made butter (yes, you really can make it yourself! See page 112). Or we have paired menu and snack ideas with many recipes, so that bread can take its rightful place at the heart of your meal. Enjoy!

FRAGRANT NETTLE & CHIVE BREAD

For most of us, thinking about nettles takes us back to childhood and getting stung. Now it's payback time! Nettles are free and a great source of iron – so why not bake with them? The combination with chives makes a warmly fragrant loaf – which we've baked here in flowerpots – as well as a dinner-table talking point.

Makes 2 small 400 g or 1 lb loaves

100 g (3 ½ oz) nettle leaves

a pinch of freshly grated nutmeg

2 tsp unsalted butter

2 heaped tsp finely chopped fresh chives

500 g (1 lb 2 oz / 3 ⅓ cups) strong white bread flour

10 g (2 tsp) fine sea salt

10 g (2 tsp) fresh yeast or 7 g (1 ½ tsp) dried or fast-action yeast

270 ml (9 ½ fl oz / 1 cup plus 1 tbsp) water

sea salt & freshly ground black pepper

TURN OVER FOR A TOASTED RAREBIT

♠ First wash the nettles thoroughly, wearing rubber gloves. Bring a pot of boiling salted water to the boil, add the nettles and blanch for two to three minutes. Leave to cool, then roughly chop the leaves, season with salt and freshly grated nutmeg, and set aside until later.

♠ Melt the butter in another pan, then toss in the chives and stir. The aim is not to cook the chives, just to warm them – this really brings out the flavour. Put the chives aside.

♠ Combine the flour, salt, chives and prepared nettles in a bowl and make a well in the centre. Crumble the yeast into the water and stir to dissolve. Add the water to the well and bring together into a dough with your hands or with a spatula. Turn the dough out on to a clean kitchen surface and knead for 10 minutes or until you achieve the windowpane effect (see page 29).

♠ Place the dough in a lightly oiled bowl, cover with a damp cloth and leave to prove for 60–90 minutes or until doubled in size. Turn the proved dough out on to a clean surface and knock it back. Divide into two equal portions, then shape it into loaves and place in two lightly oiled 400 g or 1 lb loaf tins – or flowerpots. Cover and allow to prove again for 60–80 minutes. The loaves should come to just below the rims of the tins or have increased by two-thirds.

♠ Preheat the oven to 220°C (425°F/Gas 7) and put a roasting tray in the bottom. When ready to bake, place the loaves in the oven and steam by adding ice cubes or cold water to the tray. After 25 minutes remove the loaves from the tins, then return them to the oven and cook for a further eight minutes, until golden-topped and the base of the loaf sounds hollow when tapped.

FLOWERPOT BREADS

To season new terracotta pots for baking,
wash them thoroughly and leave to dry,
then brush the insides with oil and bake
in a hot oven for 30-60 minutes. When
making your loaves, line the pots with
baking parchment so they come out easily.

CLASSIC WELSH RAREBIT

There is no better example of how bread can be turned into a meal in just minutes than this killer Welsh rarebit topping. Fast food meets comfort food – it doesn't get more satisfying than this!

4 tsp butter

20 g (¾ oz) plain (all-purpose) flour

100 ml (3 ½ fl oz) warmed milk

150 g (5 ½ oz / 1 ½ cups) coarsely grated good strong cheddar cheese

1 tsp English mustard

150 ml (5 fl oz / a scant ⅔ cup) local ale (beer)

1 tsp worcestershire sauce

4 slices nettle & chive bread (see page 46)

sea salt & freshly ground black pepper

♠ To make the topping, melt the butter in a saucepan over a low heat and stir in the flour. Gradually add the warmed milk, stirring continuously until the sauce reaches a smooth consistency. As it thickens, mix in the cheese and mustard. Remove from the heat.

♠ Boil the ale in another saucepan until it has reduced in volume by half. Add the worcestershire sauce and then combine with your cheese sauce. You should end up with a lovely, velvety mixture.

♠ Grab your slices of nettle and chive bread and toast them on one side. Spread the mix generously on the other side and place under the grill (broiler) until bubbling and starting to brown.

TRY IT WITH SOME RELISH

To add a further dimension, smear anchovy butter (see page 112) on the bread before covering with the cheese mix. Onion relish (see page 53) beneath the cheese adds a beautiful sweetness.

DUNCAN'S SPEEDY RAREBIT

Most of us can rustle up a lump of cheddar, some mayo and a jar of mustard from the fridge. Simply grate enough cheese into a bowl to cover your bread slices, add just enough mayo to make a thick mess, and then a couple of dollops of mustard. Have a taste - if you want more tanginess, add more mustard. Then get grilling. Lovely.

SEE PAGE 46 FOR THE NETTLE & CHIVE BREAD

POTATO & ROSEMARY BREAD

Potato is a great ingredient to use in bread as the natural starch reacts with the dough, giving it a wonderful soft and light crumb. This recipe is the perfect way to use up leftover mash or potato – teamed with the rosemary it makes a fantastic loaf.

TURN OVER FOR YOUR ULTIMATE STEAK SANDWICH

Makes 1 large 800 g or 2 lb loaf

½ bulb of garlic

200 g (7 oz) potatoes, peeled and cut into chunks

500 g (1 lb 2 oz / 3⅓ cups) strong white bread flour

10 g (2 tsp) fine sea salt

2 heaped tsp chopped rosemary leaves

10 g (2 tsp) fresh yeast or 7 g (1½ tsp) dried or fast-action yeast

250 ml (9 fl oz / 1 cup) water

3 tsp rapeseed or olive oil

♠ Preheat the oven to 180°C (350°F/Gas 4) and put the garlic, with its skin on, in a roasting dish. Bake for about 20 minutes or until soft. Squeeze out the flesh from three garlic cloves. You can give yourself a head start by doing this in advance and use the rest of the garlic as the perfect addition to soups and mashed potato.

♠ Meanwhile, boil the potatoes in salted water until tender. Drain and mash – or if you have some boiled potatoes or mash left over from last night's dinner, even better. (If the mash is creamy, hold back a little of the water when you mix it into the flour.)

♠ Mix the flour with the salt, rosemary, garlic and potato in a bowl and make a well in the centre. Crumble the yeast into the water and stir to dissolve. Pour the yeasted water and the oil into the well and bring together into a dough with your hands or with a spatula. At this point things may get a little messy but be persistent and continue mixing. As the flour is incorporated the dough will start to take shape.

♠ Turn the dough out on to a clean kitchen surface and knead for 10 minutes or until you achieve the windowpane effect (see page 29). Place in a lightly oiled bowl, cover with a damp cloth and leave to prove for about 60–80 minutes or until doubled in size.

♠ Turn the dough out on to a clean surface and knock it back, then allow it to rest for about five minutes. Shape the dough into a loaf as desired, or pop it into a lightly oiled large loaf tin. Cover the loaf with a damp cloth and allow to prove again for 50–60 minutes. The loaf should double in size.

♠ Preheat the oven to 220°C (425°F/Gas 7) and put a roasting tray in the bottom. When ready to bake, place the loaf in the oven and steam by adding ice cubes or cold water to the tray. Bake the loaf for 30–35 minutes, until golden and the base sounds hollow.

SAGE & ONION BREAD

For another great pairing use sage instead of rosemary and replace the potato with 100 g (3½ oz) slowly braised or roasted sliced onion. It is essential that you don't use raw onion, as this contains an enzyme that attacks the yeast.

~~GREAT~~ ULTIMATE STEAK SANDWICH
WITH SWEET ONION RELISH

THE HAND TEST

Give the steak a poke with your finger to see how firm it is, and compare this with the softness or firmness of the base of your thumb.

Heaven on a plate for us is a perfectly cooked steak, served up with potato, garlic and rosemary. So what better to use as the base for your ultimate steak sandwich than potato & rosemary bread – and then top that with home-made sweet onion relish. Outstanding! Use two slices, or cut up a whole loaf.

RARE

MEDIUM RARE

MEDIUM

WELL DONE

SEE PAGE 50 FOR POTATO & ROSEMARY BREAD

Makes 1 sandwich

1 rump or sirloin steak

2 tbsp olive oil

2 thick-cut slices of potato &
rosemary bread (see page 50)

a large handful of rocket (arugula)
or watercress

3 tsp sweet onion relish (see below),
or to taste

sea salt & freshly ground black pepper

FOR THE STEAK SANDWICH

♠ Season the steak on both sides and spread with 3 tsp of the olive oil. Place in a hot frying pan or ridged chargrill pan on a high heat to seal, then cook the steak for about five minutes on each side, depending on how rare you like it and the thickness (see the guide opposite). Remove and allow to rest.

♠ Meanwhile, toast the bread lightly. Dress the leaves with the remaining olive oil and season them. Smother one slice of toasted bread with onion relish, add the steak, cover with the dressed leaves and top with the other slice. For a slightly different kick try using wild garlic butter (see page 112) in place of the onion relish. It delivers a great garlic fragrance without being overpowering.

Makes about 4 jars

3 tsp rapeseed or olive oil

1.1 kg (2 lb 7 oz) red onions, thinly sliced

250 g (9 oz / 1⅓ cups) soft brown sugar

250 ml (9 fl oz / 1 cup) balsamic vinegar

200 g (7 oz / 1⅓ cups) cherry
tomatoes, quartered

250 g (9 oz / 1½ cups) raisins

3 tsp wholegrain mustard

sea salt & freshly ground black pepper

SWEET ONION RELISH

This onion relish is quick and easy to put together and will keep for up to a month in the fridge. The combination of the sweetness of the onion with the sharpness of the vinegar transforms any platter of cheese, cold meats or salad.

♠ Heat the oil in a large, heavy-bottomed pan on a medium heat. Add the onions and cook gently for about five minutes, stirring occasionally, until they start to soften. Stir in the brown sugar. As the onion starts to caramelise, stir in the vinegar. This will deglaze the pan, freeing any flavour in the caramel stuck to its surface.

♠ As the vinegar gently simmers, stir in the tomatoes, raisins and mustard. Continue cooking for about 15 minutes. What you should be left with is a sticky, soft, sweet relish. While the relish is still very hot, put it into sterilised jars (see page 136) and seal.

LOCAL CHEESE LOAF

With our bakery just a few miles down the road from Cheddar, in south-west England, it would be downright rude not to use this world-famous cheese. But even if you don't live on Cheddar's doorstep, there will most likely be a cheese that's made not too far away from you. So celebrate it!

Makes 2 small 400 g or 1 lb loaves

500 g (1 lb 2 oz / 3 ⅓ cups) strong white bread flour

10 g (2 tsp) fine sea salt

10 g (2 tsp) golden caster (superfine) sugar

100 g (3 ½ oz / 1 cup) grated strong local cheese, ideally a hard cheese such as cheddar

10 g (2 tsp) fresh yeast or 7 g (1 ½ tsp) dried or fast-action yeast

300 ml (10 ½ fl oz) water

♠ Combine the flour with the salt, sugar and grated cheese in a bowl and make a well in the centre. Crumble the yeast into the water and stir to dissolve. Pour the yeasted water into the well and bring together into a dough with your hands or with a spatula.

♠ Turn the dough out on to a clean kitchen surface and knead for 10 minutes or until you achieve the windowpane effect (see page 29). Place in a lightly oiled bowl, cover with a damp cloth and allow to prove for about 60 minutes or until it has doubled in size.

♠ Turn the dough out on to a clean surface and knock it back, then allow it to rest for about five minutes. Divide the rested dough into two equal portions. Shape into two nice ball loaves (see page 40) and place on a baking tray, allowing enough space so that the loaves will not touch while proving. Cover them with a damp cloth and allow to prove for another 60 minutes. They should double in size.

♠ Preheat the oven to 220°C (425°F/Gas 7) and put a roasting tray in the bottom. When ready to bake, place the loaves in the oven and steam by adding ice cubes or cold water to the tray. After about 15 minutes reduce the oven temperature to 190°C (375°F/Gas 5), as the cheese in the dough will naturally caramelise quite quickly. Continue baking for a further 15–20 minutes, until golden and the base of the loaf sounds hollow when tapped.

**TURN OVER FOR
A CHUTNEY & SALAD**

MAKE SURE IT MELTS

You want a cheese that will melt and ooze right into this loaf, rather than stay in little cheesy pockets, and one with a strong enough flavour. The taste of mild cheeses such as brie will just get lost.

TASTIEST BEETROOT

If you are roasting beetroot, for maximum flavour cook the beets whole, skins on, laid on a bed of sliced onion, fennel and orange. Cover with foil and roast in the oven at 160 C (315 F/Gas 2-3) for two to three hours. To remove the skins simply rub them off while the beetroot are still warm.

BEETROOT CHUTNEY
(& A PEAR SALAD)

SEE PAGE 54 FOR THE LOCAL CHEESE LOAF

This is your chance to reinvent the ploughman's lunch – cheese loaf, home-made chutney and crunchy salad. The beetroot chutney is a recipe Patrick stole from his mum while staying back in Ireland. After watching friends and family constantly pestering her for the recipe, he had to give it a go – now it's your turn to spread the love.

Makes 4 jars

2 tbsp olive oil

400 g (14 oz / 2 ½ cups) finely diced onion

400 g (14 oz) apple, cored and diced

450 g (1 lb / 2 ½ cups) soft brown sugar

450 ml (16 fl oz) red wine vinegar

1 kg (2 lb 4oz) cooked beetroot, diced

2 tsp sea salt

1 tsp white pepper

1 tsp finely chopped fresh root ginger

2 cinnamon sticks

6 star anise

1 tsp whole cloves

BEETROOT CHUTNEY WITH STAR ANISE & CINNAMON

♣ Heat the oil in a heavy-bottomed pan and cook the onions over a medium heat until soft. Add the diced apple and stir in the sugar and vinegar. Bring to a gentle simmer.

♣ Add the beetroot, seasoning and spices then simmer on a gentle heat for 20–30 minutes until thickened and sticky. Pour into sterilised jars (see page 136) and seal immediately. Keeps for several months in a cool, dark cupboard.

Serves 2

2 large handfuls of rocket (arugula)

1 pear, cored and thinly sliced

2 tsp olive oil

juice of ½ lemon

30 g (1 oz) parmesan cheese

freshly ground black pepper

PEAR & ROCKET SALAD

♣ Combine the rocket and sliced pear in a mixing bowl. Dress with the olive oil and lemon juice then grate over the parmesan. This salad requires no salt, just a little freshly ground black pepper.

♣ Serve the salad with chunks of the local cheese loaf (see page 54) and a big spoon of chutney (see above) on the side.

SAY CHEESE

JOHN SPENCER

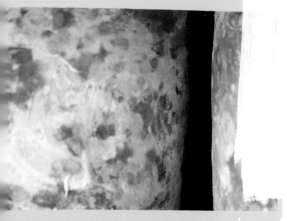

BLUE CHEESE, HONEY & WALNUT LOAF

Like the best cheeseboard, this bread combines cheese with nectary richness. The sharp, strong flavour of the blue cheese is complemented by the sweetness of the honey and the earthy walnuts. Glass of red wine or crisp, cold cider, anyone?

Makes 2 small 400 g or 1 lb loaves

500 g (1 lb 2 oz / 3⅓ cups) strong white bread flour

10 g (2 tsp) fine sea salt

15 g (3 tsp) fresh yeast or 10 g (2 tsp) dried or fast-action yeast

260 ml (9 fl oz) water

2 tsp honey

90 g (3¼ oz) blue cheese

60 g (2¼ oz / ½ cup) walnut pieces

♠ Combine the flour and salt in a bowl and make a well in the centre. Crumble the yeast into the water and stir to dissolve. Pour the yeasted water and the honey into the well and bring together into a dough with your hands or with a spatula.

♠ Turn out on to a clean kitchen surface and knead for 10 minutes or until you achieve the windowpane effect (see page 29). Crumble the cheese on to the dough and add the walnut pieces. Lightly knead these in to mix through. You just want to incorporate the cheese and walnuts evenly, without having them break up, so that the finished dough retains little pockets of cheese and walnut. (If you find your dough takes on a pink tinge, this is just the natural oils of the walnuts.)

♠ Place the dough in a lightly oiled bowl and cover with a damp cloth. Leave to prove for 60–90 minutes or until the dough has doubled in size. Turn the dough out on to a clean surface, knock it back and divide into two equal portions. For rustic-looking bread, line two bowls with floured couche cloths or tea towels. Form the dough into two balls (see page 40), generously flour the loaves and put them in the bowls with the smooth-side down and seam upwards. Prove again for about 50 minutes.

♠ Preheat the oven to 230°C (450°F/Gas 8) and put a roasting tray in the bottom. Turn the bowls over to tip the loaves out on to a baking tray lined with baking parchment. They should be seam-side down and well spaced apart. Use a baker's blade (lame) to score the top, if you like. Place the loaves in the oven and steam by adding ice cubes or cold water to the roasting tray. After 10 minutes reduce the temperature to 190°C (375°F/Gas 5). Continue baking for a further 20 minutes, until the loaves are rich golden brown and the base sounds hollow when tapped.

CHEESY TIPS

Ideally you want a blue cheese with a strong flavour that will carry through the loaf. Don't worry if you find the cheese a little strong on its own, as it will mellow out when incorporated into the dough and baked. We like to use one of two English cheeses - either Shropshire blue or Cornish blue vinny.

TURN OVER FOR A CRUNCHY CELERIAC SALAD

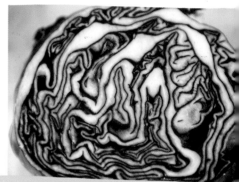

CELERIAC

SWEET & FORAGED

With a few simple tweaks and twists you can make this salad your own. Instead of walnuts you could use pecans, which are sweeter, or cobnuts, which can be foraged from parks (see page 16).

SEE PAGE 60 FOR THE BLUE CHEESE LOAF

CELERIAC & RED CABBAGE SALAD

Serves 4

¼ red cabbage, finely sliced

½ head of celeriac, peeled and cut into matchsticks

1 dessert apple, cored and diced

a handful of walnuts

a small bunch of grapes, halved

3 tsp mayonnaise

3 tsp natural yoghurt

juice of ½ lemon

1 tsp wholegrain mustard

2 handfuls of mixed salad or foraged leaves (see page 16)

sea salt & freshly ground black pepper

We've dragged the classic Waldorf salad kicking and screaming into the 21st century with the addition of red cabbage and of celeriac – a much underrated vegetable that gives this salad real bite.

♠ Mix the cabbage, celeriac, apple, walnuts and grapes in a bowl. In another bowl combine the mayonnaise, yoghurt, lemon juice and wholegrain mustard. Stir together and taste, adjusting the seasoning as required. Fold the dressing into the cabbage mixture. Serve with a mix of salad leaves, or include foraged leaves (see page 16).

♠ Serve with slices of blue cheese, honey and walnut bread (see page 60) for a light lunch.

CIDER & APPLE BREAD

This recipe is a tribute to the south-west of England, the home of great cider and birthplace of The Thoughtful Bread Company. The blend of diced apple and sweet cider produces a light and gorgeously tasty loaf. Just sit back and enjoy the wonderful apple aroma as it escapes from the oven.

TURN OVER FOR A CROQUE MONSIEUR

Makes 2 small 400 g or 1 lb loaves

500 g (1 lb 2 oz / 3⅓ cups) strong white bread flour

8 g (1½ tsp) fine sea salt

10 g (2 tsp) fresh yeast or 7 g (1½ tsp) dried or fast-action yeast

300 ml (10½ fl oz) medium cider

100 g (3½ oz) peeled and cored dessert apple, cut into 1 cm (½ in) dice

♠ Mix together the flour and salt in a bowl, then crumble in the yeast. Make a well in the centre and pour in the cider. Bring together into a dough with your hands or with a spatula.

♠ Turn the dough out on to a clean kitchen surface and knead for 10 minutes or until you achieve the windowpane effect (see page 29). Add the apple and knead lightly to incorporate. Place the dough in a lightly oiled bowl and cover with a damp cloth. Leave to prove for 60–90 minutes or until the dough has doubled in size.

♠ Turn the dough out on to a clean surface and knock it back. Divide into two equal portions, then shape it into loaves and place in two lightly oiled 400 g or 1 lb loaf tins. Leave to prove for a further 50 minutes. The dough should rise to just below the rim of the tin.

♠ Preheat the oven to 230°C (450°F/Gas 8) and put a roasting tray in the bottom. When ready to bake, place the loaves in the oven and steam by adding ice cubes or cold water to the tray. After 15 minutes reduce the temperature to 200°C (400°F/Gas 6) and bake for a further 10 minutes. Pop the loaves out of their tins and bake for another couple of minutes, until the bread is golden and sounds hollow when the base is tapped.

PERFECT COMPANIONS

Firm, crunchy dessert apples work best in this recipe. When it comes to selecting a cider you want something a little sweet and not too dry. We use a great local cider called Kingston Black.

SEE PAGE 64 FOR APPLE & CIDER BREAD

CLASSIC
CROQUE MONSIEUR

Being half French, Duncan has grown up with croque monsieur – it's an institution for him. But it didn't take much to convince Patrick that this is more than just a ham and cheese toastie – especially when made with thick slices of cider & apple bread. The apple and ham are perfect partners. Ideally you want a cheese that melts well – we use a semi-hard cow's milk cheese called Wife of Bath, made locally in Somerset. Add your own favourite for a personal touch.

Makes 1 sandwich

2 thick-cut slices of cider & apple bread (see page 64)

3 tsp butter

1 tsp dijon mustard

2 slices of cooked ham

50 g (1 ¾ oz) of your favourite cheese, thinly sliced

a few drops of worcestershire sauce

♠ Lightly toast the bread on one side, then spread the toasted side with half the butter and the teaspoon of mustard. Cover one slice with the ham and top generously with cheese. Season with a few drops of worcestershire sauce and form into a sandwich.

♠ Spread the remaining butter on the untoasted sides of bread. Pop under a hot grill (broiler) and toast on both sides. The croque monsieur should be golden and oozing with melted cheese. Enjoy warm or savour cold as the ideal lunch snack on the go.

CROQUE TWISTS

→ Top with a fried egg to make croque madame.

→ Go retro by substituting a tin of sardines for the ham.

→ Spread the bread with a layer of olive tapenade instead of mustard.

MULTI-GRAIN BURGER BUNS

Sometimes white or brown just isn't enough, sometimes the occasion calls for a little more body. Our multi-grain recipe takes basic white dough and stuffs it with brown rice, pearl barley and oats. It makes the best burger buns for the barbecue.

Makes 10 burger buns

40 g (1½ oz / ¼ cup) pearl barley

40 g (1½ oz / ¼ cup) brown rice

400 g (14 oz / 2⅔ cups) strong white bread flour

100 g (3½ oz / ⅔ cup) strong wholemeal flour

15 g (3 tsp) fine sea salt

20 g (4 tsp) soft brown sugar

25 g (1 oz / ¼ cup) jumbo or porridge oats, plus extra for sprinkling

20 g (4 tsp) fresh yeast or 10 g (2 tsp) dried or fast-action yeast

250 ml (9 fl oz / 1 cup) water

1 egg

5 tsp rapeseed or olive oil

♠ First cook the pearl barley and brown rice. Rinse the grains in cold water and place in two separate saucepans. To the pearl barley add the same volume of water and a pinch of salt. Brown rice tends to cook more slowly and needs more water, so add twice the volume of water as rice, along with a pinch of salt.

♠ Bring both pans to the boil on a high heat then turn right down, cover with a lid and cook until the water has been absorbed and the grains are soft. Leave to cool with the lid on.

♠ Mix together the flours, salt and sugar, cooked barley and rice, and raw oats. The sugar will bring out the flavour of the grains. Crumble the yeast into the water and stir to dissolve. Make a well in the dry ingredients and crack the egg into it. Add the yeasted water and the oil and bring together into a dough with your hands or with a spatula.

♠ Turn the dough out on to a clean kitchen surface and knead for about 10 minutes or until you achieve the windowpane effect (see page 29). Don't worry if the dough is a bit wet initially, as it takes a little time for the grains to absorb the water. Place the dough in a lightly oiled bowl, cover with a damp cloth and leave to prove for 60–90 minutes or until doubled in size.

♠ Turn the dough out on to a clean surface and knock it back. Portion it evenly into 10 buns and roll into nice small balls (see page 40). Place on a lightly greased baking tray and prove again for 60–90 minutes, until doubled in size.

♠ Preheat the oven to 230°C (450°F/Gas 8). Mist the tops of the buns with water and sprinkle with more oats. Bake for 14–16 minutes, until the buns are golden and well risen.

BUN SIZES

100 g / 3½ oz is a nice size for a full-size burger bun, but you could halve that and make mini buns for children.

TURN OVER FOR BARBECUED VEGGIE STACKS ➤

FOR THE MEAT EATERS

If you do like a beef burger, simply load it up with the veg and dressed leaves on top.

BARBECUED VEGGIE STACKS
WITH HONEY MUSTARD DRESSING

SEE PAGE 68 FOR MULTI-GRAIN BUNS

Serves 4

1 red (bell) pepper,
deseeded and quartered

1 courgette (zucchini), sliced at an angle

1 red onion, peeled and quartered

olive oil to coat the vegetables

1 tsp chopped thyme leaves

1 garlic clove, thinly sliced

4 slices of halloumi cheese

1 beef tomato, sliced

a handful of watercress

sea salt & freshly ground black pepper

For the dressing:

50 ml (1 ¾ fl oz) olive oil

1 tsp honey

1 tsp wholegrain mustard

juice of ½ lemon

For this veggie alternative to traditional burgers we built an impromptu garden barbie – some bricks and stone blocks, a shelf from the oven and locally sourced charcoal (great if you can find it). The honey dressing adds sweetness, and salty grilled halloumi cheese gives texture and contrast.

♠ Put the pepper, courgette and onion in a bowl, drizzle with a little olive oil and season with the thyme and garlic, and salt and pepper. Place on the barbecue and cook until tender, about five minutes on each side (the onions may take a couple more minutes). Rub the halloumi with a little oil and grill on the barbecue for about a minute on each side, until turning rich golden brown.

♠ Meanwhile, make the dressing. Whisk together all the ingredients in a bowl and season to taste. Remove the vegetables from the barbecue and toss them in the honey mustard dressing.

♠ To assemble the veggie stack cut a bun in half and layer it up with the barbecued vegetables. Top with a slice of tomato, the grilled halloumi and some peppery watercress, plus a drizzle of any leftover dressing.

RUSTIC WHITE BAGUETTE

There is just something irresistible about a baguette, especially when it's fresh out of the oven. There's always the urge to tear straight into it. No bread book would be complete without the mighty baguette – so here's our version.

Makes 2 baguettes

150 g (5 ½ oz) potato

500 g (1 lb 2 oz / 3 ⅓ cups) strong white bread flour

15 g (3 tsp) fine sea salt

10 g (2 tsp) fresh yeast or 7 g (1 ½ tsp) dried or fast-action yeast

225 ml (7 ¾ fl oz) water

4 tsp rapeseed or olive oil

♠ Boil the potatoes in salted water until tender. Drain and mash — or if you have mash from last night's dinner, even better. (If the mash is creamy, hold back a little water when you mix it into the flour.)

♠ Combine the flour, salt and mashed potato in a bowl and form a well in the centre. Crumble the yeast into the water and stir to dissolve, then add the yeasted water and oil to the well. Bring together into a dough with a wooden spoon or with a spatula. Turn the dough out on to a clean kitchen surface and knead for about 10 minutes or until you achieve the windowpane effect (see page 29). The dough should be soft and supple. Place in a lightly oiled bowl, cover with a damp cloth and leave to prove for 60–80 minutes or until doubled in size. Turn the dough out and knock it back, then divide in half.

♠ To form a baguette, flatten the dough evenly into a rectangle, then roll it up into a cylindrical shape. It should resemble a sausage about 30 cm (12 in) long. Using the palms of your hands and starting in the middle, roll the dough to lengthen the baguette, moving from the middle to the outer edges, until it is about 50 cm (20 in) long – but check that it will fit in your oven! Place each baguette on a lightly oiled baking tray and cover with a damp cloth. Prove for 50–60 minutes.

♠ Preheat the oven to 230°C (450°F/Gas 8) and place a roasting tray in the bottom. Before baking lightly dust each baguette with flour and use a baker's blade (lame) or a sharp serrated knife to score the top with a series of cuts at a slight angle. Place the loaves in the oven and steam by adding ice cubes or cold water to the tray. Bake for 35 minutes, rotating halfway through to ensure even cooking. The baguettes should be crisp and golden.

TURN OVER FOR A HAM HOCK TERRINE

SEE PAGE 72 FOR THE RUSTIC BAGUETTE

TOO SALTY?

To check the saltiness of your ham hocks, cut off a little piece of the raw ham and cook in boiling water until tender, then taste. If it's too salty, soak the ham hocks for a few hours in several changes of cold water.

HAM HOCK TERRINE

The idea of making a terrine might seem daunting but we are here to show that it's a lot easier than you think. This terrine is basically a mosaic of layered ham and can be dressed up or down for any occasion – it'll put a smile on the face of even the most critical foodie. Hocks are packed with flavour and cheap as chips, so speak to your butcher.

Serves 4-6

3 ham hocks

3 carrots, peeled and roughly chopped

2 sticks celery, roughly chopped

1 white onion, roughly chopped

1 tsp peppercorns

1 tsp coriander seeds

1 bay leaf

2 tbsp chopped fresh parsley

1 tsp capers, finely chopped

4 baby gherkins (pickles), finely chopped

sea salt & freshly ground black pepper

♠ Place the ham hocks in a large saucepan, cover with water and bring to the boil. Simmer for five minutes – you will find that all the impurities come to the surface. Remove the ham hocks and rinse in cold water, return to a clean saucepan, cover with water and bring to the boil again. Reduce to a gentle simmer and add the vegetables, peppercorns, coriander seeds and bay leaf. Cover with a lid and simmer on a gentle heat for 2½–3 hours, until the meat is tender and easily pulls away from the bone.

♠ Remove the ham hocks and set aside to cool. Strain the cooking liquor through a fine sieve and return it to a clean saucepan. Place on a medium heat and boil until reduced by half. Peel the fat from the ham hocks and discard. Flake the meat off the bone with your fingers and put in a bowl.

♠ Add the parsley, capers and gherkins and check the seasoning, although you may not need anything further. Add 4 tbsp (60 ml/2 fl oz) of the cooking liquor and stir in to bind everything together.

♠ Line a terrine mould – or a 400 g or 1 lb loaf tin – with two layers of clingfilm, allowing for about a 5 cm (2 in) overhang all round. Fill the terrine mould with the meat. Press the mixture down and pour in the remaining cooking liquor until it just covers the top.

♠ Fold over the clingfilm and put the terrine in the fridge overnight to set, placing a heavy weight on top.

♠ To serve remove the terrine from the mould, unwrap the clingfilm and cut into slices with a sharp knife. Delicious with a tangy chutney or piccalilli and a freshly made crusty baguette.

IRISH SODA BREAD

What can one say about soda bread except that it is quick, easy and simply delicious. I forced this recipe on Duncan from the start and it just happens that this was one of our first breads to win an award – not that I'm biased, as a proud Irishman. The main difference with soda bread is that it uses bicarbonate of soda to make the bubbles, not yeast.

Traditionally the soft soda bread dough is formed into a round and cut with a cross before baking. This recipe calls for a very wet mix that is baked in a tin; sometimes this version is known as wheaten bread.

♠ The method could not be simpler. Preheat the oven to 200°C (400°F/Gas 6). Mix the flour, salt, sugar and bicarbonate of soda and make a well in the centre. Add the milk, oil and red wine vinegar and stir to mix. Don't worry — the mixture is supposed to resemble a thick porridge, and everything will be fine.

♠ Divide between two lightly oiled 400 g or 1 lb loaf tins and bake for 35 minutes. The bread is cooked when the tip of a knife inserted in the centre of the loaf comes out clean. Cool on a wire rack.

TURN OVER FOR SPICED PARSNIP SOUP ➤

SEE PAGE 76 FOR THE IRISH SODA BREAD

SEASONAL SOUPS

Try spring vegetables, a puréed pea soup, summer roasted tomato with basil, or butternut squash.

SPICED
PARSNIP & CORIANDER SOUP
(WITH CURRY OIL)

Serves 4

3 medium parsnips, peeled & halved

1 tsp ground coriander

45 ml (1 ½ fl oz) sunflower oil

1 garlic clove, finely chopped

1 onion, finely chopped

1 leek, finely chopped

2 sprigs thyme

1 litre (35 fl oz / 4 cups)
chicken or vegetable stock

sea salt & freshly
ground black pepper

For the curry oil:

100 ml (3 ½ fl oz) sunflower oil,
plus 3 tsp

1 shallot, diced

½ tsp ground coriander

½ tsp turmeric

½ tsp ground cumin

Soup is a bread's best friend. The secret to a great one, we believe, is using what's in season. For winter here in Somerset that means parsnips. So we have chosen a spiced soup with a warming curry oil. But don't feel confined to our ingredients – let Mother Nature write your shopping list.

♠ First make the curry oil. You can do this in advance and the oil will be a great addition to your larder, keeping for several weeks. Heat 3 tsp of sunflower oil in a saucepan and gently cook the shallot until soft. Add the spices and cook for a further two minutes, then pour in the rest of the sunflower oil and warm gently. Remove from the heat and leave to cool. Infuse overnight then pass through a sieve.

♠ For the soup, preheat the oven to 160°C (315°F/Gas 2–3). Season the parsnips with the ground coriander and put them in a roasting tray with 3 tsp of oil. Roast for 30 minutes or until tender.

♠ Heat the remaining oil in a saucepan over a medium heat and add the garlic, onion and leek. Cook gently until tender but not coloured. Add the sprigs of thyme and roasted parsnip, then pour in the stock and simmer for 20 minutes. Blend the soup with a hand blender and season to taste.

♠ Serve the creamed soup with a drizzle of curry oil and freshly baked soda bread.

LUNCHBOX SAVOURY SODA BREAD MUFFINS

Makes 12 muffins

500 g (1 lb 2 oz / 3 ⅓ cups) plain (all-purpose) white flour

5 g (1 tsp) fine sea salt

15 g (3 tsp) bicarbonate of soda (baking soda)

125 g (4 ½ oz) feta cheese

5 tsp rapeseed or olive oil

3 tsp honey

5 tsp red wine vinegar

300 ml (10 ½ fl oz) water

150 g (5 ½ oz) cooked beetroot, diced

100 g (3 ½ oz / ⅔ cup) cherry tomatoes, halved

melted butter for greasing

These are bread's take on fast food. Versatile and baked in minutes, the sweet beetroot, salty feta and juicy tomatoes make them a ridiculously easy-to-make and hugely satisfying snack.

♠ Combine the flour, salt and bicarbonate of soda in a bowl. Crumble in the feta cheese, add the oil, honey, vinegar and water and mix everything together with a wooden spoon or spatula. Lightly incorporate the diced beetroot.

♠ Preheat the oven to 200°C (400°F/Gas 6) and grease a muffin tray with melted butter. Take a portion of the mixture a little bigger than a golf ball, press two or three halved tomatoes into it, form into a rough ball and place in the muffin tray.

♠ Fill the muffin tray and bake in the oven for 15 minutes, until the soda bread muffins are risen and golden.

STONE-BAKED
↓
FLAT BREADS

Makes about 8 flat breads

500 g (1 lb 2 oz / 3⅓ cups) strong white bread flour

10 g (2 tsp) fine sea salt

50 g (1¾ oz) unsalted butter, softened

15 g (3 tsp) fresh yeast or 10 g (2 tsp) dried or fast-action yeast

200 ml (7 fl oz / ¾ cup plus 1 tbsp) milk

1 egg, lightly beaten

60 ml (2 fl oz / ¼ cup) olive oil

semolina for dusting

Garlic & cheese topping:

8 garlic cloves, peeled

5 g (1 tsp) sea salt

150 g (5½ oz / 1½ cups) finely grated parmesan cheese

olive oil to blend

Chilli & cheese topping:

2 tsp dried chilli flakes (we know it seems a lot but don't worry)

6 garlic cloves, peeled

150 g (5½ oz / 1½ cups) finely grated parmesan cheese

sea salt

olive oil to blend

Olive oil & herb topping:

50 ml (1¾ fl oz) olive oil

1 tsp dried oregano

sea salt & ground black pepper

One of the many things we love about bread is that it does not always have to come in the shape of a loaf. Flat breads are popular the world over and are easily made at home. We have included a few different toppings, which should help you cater for all tastes, from aromatic herb to nice and spicy.

♠ You can make the cheese toppings in advance. For the garlic and cheese topping, blitz all the ingredients in a food processor to make a paste. For the chilli and cheese topping, blitz the chilli and garlic with a little oil for a minute or two, then add the cheese and enough olive oil to form a smooth paste.

♠ To make the flat breads, combine the flour and salt in a bowl and rub in the butter with your fingertips until the mixture resembles fine breadcrumbs. Make a well in the centre. Crumble the yeast into the milk and stir to dissolve, then add the yeasted milk, egg and olive oil to the well and bring together into a dough with your hands or with a spatula. You are looking for a nice, soft, supple dough. Add a little additional milk if required.

♠ Turn the dough out on to a clean kitchen surface and knead for 10 minutes or until you achieve the windowpane effect (see page 29). Put into a lightly oiled bowl, cover with a damp cloth and leave to prove for 60 minutes or until the dough has doubled in size.

♠ Turn out the dough on to a clean surface and knock it back, then cut it into 12 equal pieces – about 100 g (3½ oz) makes a nice individual portion. Roll each piece into a ball and arrange on a floured work surface or baking tray, allowing enough room so that

PIZZA STONE

If you don't have a commercial oven to hand like us, we really recommend using a pizza stone for the best results.

TURN OVER FOR EASY CHICKEN CURRY

the rolls will not touch as they expand. Cover with a damp cloth and leave to prove for another 40 minutes.

♣ Preheat the oven to its highest setting and heat up a pizza stone. You will need the oven to reach at least 240°C (475°F/Gas 8). If you don't have a pizza stone, put your heaviest baking tray into the oven, bottom surface upwards.

♣ Dust a clean surface with semolina. Form the flat breads by flattening a ball of dough slightly with the palm of your hand, then either roll it out with a rolling pin or hold it and work it thinner with your fingers: gently pull the dough as you move it round, so it is evenly flattened and forms a circle or oval shape about 5 mm (¼ in) thick and 20 cm (8 in) in diameter.

♣ Top each flat bread generously with your preferred topping and place on the pizza stone in the oven — they will take only five to six minutes to puff up and cook. You will need to cook them in several batches.

♣ Flat breads can be eaten warm or cold. They also freeze well — you can bring them back to life with a couple of minutes in a warm oven.

NOT HOT ENOUGH?

If you like your curry to have a little more power, feel free to raise the heat with a few extra chillies.

EASY
CHICKEN CURRY

Put down the takeaway menu, it's time to make your own. Our recipe is packed with flavour rather than heat and (we hope) will become a firm favourite in your cooking repertoire. The paste is so simple, can be made in advance and will keep for several weeks in the fridge.

Serves 4

8 chicken thighs

2 white onions, finely sliced

2 tsp unsalted butter

500 ml (17 fl oz / 2 cups) chicken stock

400 ml (14 oz) tinned
coconut milk

200 g (7 oz) fine green beans, cut into
2.5 cm (1 in) lengths

For the Thai green curry paste:

1 tsp cumin seeds

1 tsp coriander seeds

2 garlic cloves, peeled

5 cm (2 in) piece of root ginger

2 fresh green chillies

1 stick of lemongrass

1 green (bell) pepper,
roughly chopped

a bunch of coriander (cilantro)

juice of 1 lime

2 tbsp sesame oil

1 tsp sea salt

♠ First make the paste — the day before if you can. Toast the cumin and coriander seeds in a dry frying pan for a couple of minutes, then put the seeds and all the rest of the ingredients in a food processor and whiz. Don't even pick the coriander leaves — we want the stems and all (do wash any roots, though). It's that simple.

♠ Time permitting, marinate the chicken thighs in 1 heaped tbsp of the curry paste. Get your hands in and make sure the chicken is well coated. Leave in the fridge for two hours, or overnight if possible.

♠ To make the curry sauce, sweat the onions with the butter in a saucepan over a medium heat, until soft and golden. Add 3 tbsp of the curry paste. Cook for five minutes, until fragrant, then add the chicken stock. Leave to simmer for 10–15 minutes. Add the coconut milk and leave to simmer on a low heat for 30 minutes while you cook the chicken thighs.

♠ Preheat the oven to 180°C (350°F/Gas 4). Heat an oven-proof frying pan on a medium heat and place the chicken thighs in it, skin-side down. As the chicken cooks, it will release natural fat from under the skin — simply pour this off. Turn the heat right down and cook the chicken slowly for at least 15–20 minutes, still with the skin-side down. This will give you wonderful crisp chicken. Turn the thighs over and finish cooking in the oven for about 15 minutes.

♠ Five minutes before serving, drop the green beans into the curry sauce. Serve the curry sauce with the chicken thighs, rice and some wonderful home-made flat breads.

SEE PAGE 82 FOR STONE-BAKED FLAT BREADS

WALCOT RFC

CRUNCHY CRACKER BREAD

Here is a simple recipe for making your very own crackers at home – great as a savoury snack, for friends and family to nibble on throughout the day. The great thing about these crackers is that they can be rolled out and cut any way you like, so this is a chance to really express yourself.

Enough for 100 crackers

500 g (1 lb 2 oz / 3 ⅓ cups) strong white bread flour

12 g (2½ tsp) fine sea salt

10 g (2 tsp) fresh yeast or 7 g (1½ tsp) dried or fast-action yeast

250 g (9 fl oz / 1 cup) water

2 tsp honey

40 ml (1¼ fl oz) rapeseed or olive oil

To garnish the crackers:

sea salt & cracked black pepper

poppy seeds

sesame seeds

caraway seeds

cumin seeds

paprika

(or anything else that needs using up)

♠ Mix together the flour and salt in a bowl and make a well in the centre. Crumble the yeast into the water and stir to dissolve. Add the honey and oil to the well, then pour in three-quarters of the yeasted water – hold a little back as you may not need it all. Bring together into a dough with your hands or with a spatula, adding more of the yeasted water if needed. This dough should be firm but not dry.

♠ Turn the dough out on to a clean kitchen surface and knead for 10 minutes or until you achieve the windowpane effect (see page 29). Place the kneaded dough in a lightly oiled bowl and cover with a damp cloth. Leave to prove for about 90 minutes, or until doubled in size. Knock back the dough and either use straightaway or store in the fridge until needed.

♠ Preheat the oven to 180°C (350°F/Gas 4) and line a baking tray with baking parchment. Cut off a small amount of dough to work with.

♠ The secret to a great cracker is getting the dough as thin as you can – if possible so you can see through it. Start rolling out the dough, gradually getting it thinner. From time to time, lift it up over your hand or arm before laying it back down. Reflour the surface if necessary to prevent the dough from sticking. As you roll the dough it will start to shrink back in. When it does, leave it for a couple of minutes to relax – you'll use half the amount of effort.

♠ Once it is thin enough, cut your crackers. You can shape them any way you like: big, small, round or square. Use a sharp knife and try to cut in a single motion so as not to pull or tear the dough. Or else bake the crackers as a large sheet, which can be snapped and shared between friends once cooked.

♠ Lay the crackers out on the baking tray and mist with a little water, then add your choice of toppings. Remember with spices that a little goes a long way. Bake the crackers for 10–12 minutes – keep an eye on them and remove them when they turn lightly golden. Cool and serve on their own, or with the dips over the page.

ROLLING OUT

We generally find it easier to roll and cut the cracker dough in smaller amounts, but if you make a large quantity of cracker dough like this you can wrap the rest in clingfilm and freeze it. This dough goes a long way - a golfball-sized piece will give a dozen crackers.

TURN OVER FOR THREE CRACKER DIPS

3 DIPS FOR YOUR CRACKERS

Bring that deli experience to your dinner table or picnic blanket. What good is a cracker without a dip?

CHEDDAR, SUNFLOWER & WILD GARLIC PESTO

A good strong cheese works best for this Thoughtful Bread Company take on the Italian classic. Sunflower seeds are a cheap alternative to pine nuts and give a rich flavour, while wild garlic is plentiful in the spring woodlands where we are based (see page 16). You could use basil or wild rocket (arugula) instead.

♠ Crumble the cheese into a food processor and blitz with the sunflower seeds and wild garlic leaves. Gradually mix in the oil and lemon juice, and season to taste.

CASHEW NUT & WATER MINT CHUTNEY

We use foraged water mint for this tangy dip, but any mint (except super-strong spearmint) will work fine.

♠ Whiz all the ingredients in a food processor, taste and adjust the seasoning if you need to.

ALMOST-INSTANT HUMMUS

♠ Put the chickpeas, lemon juice, shallot and garlic in a food processor and blitz until you have a smoothish paste. Add the olive oil gradually, until the paste is soft and spoonable. Season to taste.

SEE PAGE 88 FOR CRUNCHY CRACKER BREAD

ENGLISH → MUFFINS

Where would the breakfast table be without English muffins? These savoury, yeasted muffins are cooked on a griddle or in a frying pan, then we like to finish them off in the oven. Made from a soft, enriched dough, when cut in half and smothered in butter they are something that kids – well, not just kids – love to eat.

Makes 12 muffins

500 g (1 lb 2 oz / 3⅓ cups) strong white bread flour

15 g (3 tsp) golden caster (superfine) sugar

10 g (2 tsp) salt

5 tsp unsalted butter, softened

15 g (3 tsp) fresh yeast or 10 g (2 tsp) dried or fast-action yeast

300 ml (10 ½ fl oz) milk

olive oil & butter for frying

♠ Mix together the flour, sugar and salt in a bowl and rub in the butter with your fingertips until the mixture resembles fine breadcrumbs. Make a well in the centre. Crumble the yeast into the milk so that it dissolves, then add the yeasted milk to the well and bring the dough together with your hands or with a spatula. You are looking for a nice, soft, supple dough. Add a little more milk if required.

♠ Turn the dough out on to a clean kitchen surface and knead for 10 minutes or until you achieve the windowpane effect (see page 29). Put back into a lightly oiled bowl, cover with a damp cloth and leave to prove for 60 minutes or until the dough has doubled in size.

♠ Preheat the oven to 200°C (400°F/Gas 6). Turn the dough out on to a clean surface, knock it back and cut it into 12 equal pieces. Roll each piece into a ball, then arrange on a floured work surface or baking tray, allowing enough room so that the rolls will not touch as they rise. Cover with a damp cloth and leave to prove again for 30 minutes.

♠ Place a large, heavy-based frying pan on a medium heat and add a drizzle of olive oil and a knob of butter. When the butter has melted take two or three dough balls, depending on the size of your pan, and cook them for about two minutes on each side, or until lightly golden. As the muffins cook they will level off to take on that characteristic English muffin shape.

♠ Transfer each muffin from the pan to a baking tray and place directly in the oven to cook for 10 minutes. Do not wait until all the muffins are ready to put them in the oven – they mustn't be left to sit around as the cooking process has begun. Repeat the process with the remaining muffins, transferring each to a wire rack to cool once cooked.

TURN OVER FOR EGGS BENEDICT

RESCUING A HOLLANDAISE

If your sauce has thickened too much add a little warm water. If it has split or curdled, it can be revived. Bring 2 tbsp of cream to the boil in a clean saucepan. Slowly pour it on to the split hollandaise, whisking all the time, then remove from the heat.

Don't throw away any unused sauce: you can keep it overnight in the fridge. To warm it through, whisk it in a bowl over a pan of gently simmering water. Add some chopped tarragon and you have a béarnaise sauce, an ideal accompaniment to steak (see page 52). Breakfast and dinner from the same sauce – definitely worth the effort.

EGGS BENEDICT

This has to be the ultimate breakfast – keep your Irish breakfast or your full English: there is only one king of the breakfast table. Whether as a hangover cure or an indulgent treat, a toasted English muffin, covered with ham or bacon, topped with a poached egg and finished with hollandaise sauce is difficult to beat. If the hollandaise seems intimidating, we have included some tips for success!

Serves 2

2 English muffins (see page 92)

6 slices of streaky bacon

2 free-range eggs

3 tsp vinegar & a pinch of salt for the poaching water

For the hollandaise sauce:

150 g (5½ oz) unsalted butter

3 egg yolks

a pinch of fine sea salt

juice of ½ lemon

3 tsp white wine vinegar

SEE PAGE 92 FOR YOUR ENGLISH MUFFINS

♠ First clarify the butter for the hollandaise. Put the butter in a bowl over a saucepan of simmering water. As the butter melts the solids separate; if you heat it gently enough these will sit at the bottom, so you can pour off the golden liquid, discarding the solids.

♠ To make the hollandaise sauce, bring a small saucepan of water to a gentle simmer. Whisk the egg yolks in a bowl and add the salt and 3 tsp of hot water from the pan. Place the bowl over the simmering water and continue to whisk steadily, adding the lemon juice and white wine vinegar. Slowly pour in 100 ml (3½ fl oz) of the clarified butter in a trickle – don't add it all at once, but gradually, making sure to whisk all the time. As the butter is incorporated, the sauce will thicken. Once all the butter has been added, remove from the heat and adjust the seasoning, whisking in a touch more vinegar if you prefer your sauce sharper. You can make the hollandaise in advance and cover it with clingfilm to sit beside the stove and keep warm until needed.

♠ Cut each muffin in half and toast. Place the streaky bacon under the grill (broiler) and cook until crisp, then poach the eggs.

♠ The secret to poaching an egg, amazingly, is all down to the egg. Fresh eggs will hold together much better in the water. Fill a saucepan with about 5 cm (2 in) of water and bring to the boil. Add the vinegar and a pinch of salt – the vinegar helps to set the protein in the egg. Crack your egg into a cup, and just as you gently lay the egg into the pan, turn the water down to a simmer. For perfectly soft eggs poach for three minutes.

♠ Assemble each plate with an English muffin and three rashers of crisp bacon. Sit a poached egg on top and ladle over a generous serving of hollandaise. To brown, pop under the grill (broiler) or use a chef's blowtorch. If you like, swap the bacon for some wilted spinach and you will have yourself eggs florentine.

BRUNCH BAGELS

TURN OVER FOR A CORIANDER CRAYFISH TOPPING

What's unique about a bagel is the way it is cooked. The dough is first submerged in boiling water then finished in the oven, creating a dense, chewy inside with a crisp exterior. But, you might ask: why a hole? The answer is that it ensures even cooking.

Makes 12 bagels

750 g (1 lb 10 oz / 5 cups) strong white bread flour

15 g (3 tsp) fine sea salt

15 g (3 tsp) fresh yeast or 10 g (2 tsp) dried or fast-action yeast

375 ml (13 fl oz / 1½ cups) water

65 g (2¼ oz / 7 tsp) honey

♠ Mix together the flour and salt in a bowl and make a well in the centre. Crumble the yeast into the water and stir to dissolve, then add the yeasted water and the honey to the well. Bring together into a dough with your hands or with a spatula, then turn the dough out on to a clean kitchen surface and knead for 10 minutes or until you achieve the windowpane effect (see page 29).

♠ The dough should have a firm texture. The reason for this is that it needs to be strong enough to stand up against the boiling water when cooked. Place in a lightly oiled bowl, cover with a damp cloth and leave to prove for 60 minutes or until the dough has doubled in size.

♠ Transfer the dough to a clean surface and knock it back. Divide into 12 equal portions and roll each one into a neat, tight ball. Allow the dough to rest for five minutes, then flatten each ball down evenly with the palm of your hand. Using your thumb, push through the centre to create a hole. Slowly widen the hole using your finger while maintaining the circular shape. Dust the bagel in flour to stop the dough coming back together. Place on a floured baking tray, cover with a damp cloth and leave to prove again for 30 minutes.

♠ Preheat the oven to 200°C (400°F/Gas 6). Take your widest saucepan, half fill it with water, add a good pinch of salt and bring to the boil, then reduce the temperature to a simmer.

♠ Take each bagel and gently drop it into the simmering water. You may need to cook the bagels in batches, depending on the size of your pan. Be sure to leave enough room in the pan to allow them to expand slightly. Cook for two minutes on each side.

♠ Line a baking tray with baking parchment. Remove the first batch of bagels from the water and place them on the tray. Add any garnishes (see opposite), then bake in the oven for 12–15 minutes, until lightly golden. Repeat with the remaining bagels.

SEEDS & GARNISHES

You can garnish the bagels with linseeds, sesame seeds, poppy seeds, onion seeds or a little sea salt, or leave them plain. Add the garnishes as soon as they come out of the water.

CATCH YOUR LUNCH

Food for free doesn't come better than this! Crayfish can be caught with a basic improvised net like Duncan's (plenty of ideas on the internet) and in some areas you may well be doing the environment as well as your lunch plate a favour.

In the 1970s the North American signal crayfish was introduced into UK waters. Now these crayfish are considered a pest – so much so, in fact, that it is illegal, once caught, to return them to the water because of the damage they do to the native British species and to the riverbanks. So why not take it a step further and catch some to cook with?

To fish for signal crayfish in the UK, apply to the Environment Agency for a free licence. They'll send you a guide book to help identify which are the baddies and which are the goodies. So get trapping!

LIME & CORIANDER CRAYFISH

SEE PAGE 96 FOR BRUNCH BAGELS

Serves 2

3 tsp olive oil

100 g (3 ½ oz) raw crayfish tails or prawns

1 fresh red chilli, de-seeded and finely sliced

3 tsp unsalted butter

2 fresh tomatoes, chopped

juice of ½ lime

1 tsp chopped fresh coriander (cilantro)

sea salt

Duncan brought me back a bucket load of wild crayfish that he had caught one morning, which I transformed into a bagel topping packed with zingy flavours. You could use prawns instead.

♠ Heat a frying pan over a medium heat and add the olive oil. Put in the crayfish tails or prawns and season with salt and the chilli. Fry for no more than two minutes, until the flesh has just turned opaque (it's easy to overcook them, so keep a watch). Add the butter to the pan to create a sauce and finish with the tomatoes, lime juice and coriander. Serve piled on a warm toasted bagel.

FOCACCIA
— OF —
1000 TOPPINGS

Focaccia is pizza's big brother. Enriched with olive oil, rolled out flat and shaped with your fingertips, it is great served alongside a meal, as a meal in itself, or as sandwich bread. The toppings provide an opportunity to get creative with whatever you have lying around.

Makes 4 focaccias 25 cm (10 in) in diameter

500 g (1 lb 2 oz / 3 ⅓ cups) strong white bread flour

10 g (2 tsp) fine sea salt

10 g (2 tsp) fresh yeast or 7 g (1 ½ tsp) dried or fast-action yeast

200 ml (7 fl oz) water

100 ml (3 ½ fl oz) olive oil, plus 2 tbsp to pour on the focaccia

sea salt flakes & freshly ground black pepper

♠ Mix together the flour and salt in a bowl and make a well in the centre. Crumble the yeast into the water and stir to dissolve, then add it to the well, along with the 100 ml (3 ½ fl oz) of olive oil. Bring together into a dough with your hands or with a spatula, then turn the dough out on to a clean kitchen surface and knead for 10 minutes or until you achieve the windowpane effect (see page 29). The dough should be soft and elastic. Cover with a damp cloth and leave to prove for 60 minutes or until the dough has doubled in size.

♠ After it has proved, knock back the dough, cut it into four equal pieces and form each piece into a ball. Lightly press each ball with your fingertips to flatten it, slowly working the dough out like a pizza base. The dough has a natural tendency to shrink, so it's best to work it in stages. Roughly shape the first piece of dough, place it to one side and allow it to rest as you work on the next piece.

♠ Continue pressing and forming the dough circles until they are about 1 cm (½ in) thick. The dough should resemble a thick-crust pizza base. Push your fingertips into the surface to create dimples, then pour on the remaining olive oil, smoothing it over the surface and pushing in more dimples if needed.

♠ Add your chosen toppings, grind over some black pepper and sprinkle with sea salt flakes. Put on to baking trays lined with baking parchment, cover with a damp cloth and leave to prove for 30 minutes.

♠ Preheat the oven to 200°C (400°F/Gas 6). Bake the focaccias for about 20 minutes, until lightly golden.

FRESH HERBS

You can also put chopped fresh herbs into your dough — simply add to the flour at the mixing stage.

Try: marjoram, basil, oregano, sage, rosemary.

If you don't have any growing at home, rosemary is particularly good for a spot of 'urban foraging'. Next time you're out and about have a look at public flowerbeds or gardens. Ask the park keepers or owners if you can do a spot of light pruning…

Topping 1:

10 cherry tomatoes, halved

a small handful of basil, leaves picked

½ ball of mozzarella, roughly torn

Topping 2:

4 thin slices salami, chorizo or other cured meat, roughly torn

½ green (bell) pepper, thinly sliced

2 spring onions (scallions), shredded

Topping 3:

3 cloves garlic, crushed and mixed with 2 tbsp olive oil

1 tbsp finely grated parmesan cheese, mixed into the garlic and olive oil

2 sprigs rosemary, leaves picked and roughly chopped

Topping 4:

100 g (3 ½ oz / 1 cup) thinly sliced mushrooms, fried in 10 g (2 tsp) butter until lightly golden

3 tsp chopped sage

RYE CRACKERS

TURN OVER FOR SALMON TARTARE

For something a little different to share around, try these wheat-free crackers made from rye. Naturally lower in gluten, this flour can sometimes be difficult to turn into a loaf but really lends itself well to making these crackers. With their unmistakable flavour, they crisp up to make the perfect party food.

Makes 12 crackers

400 g (14 oz) rye flour

5 g (1 tsp) fine sea salt

10 g (2 tsp) fresh yeast or 7 g (1½ tsp) dried or fast-action yeast

10 g (1 tsp) honey

350 ml (12 fl oz) water

♠ Combine the flour and salt in a bowl and make a well in the centre. Crumble the yeast in the water, stir to dissolve and pour the yeasted water and honey into the well. Bring the mix together using a spatula — it should form a stiff, wet dough.

♠ Instead of kneading, simply cover the dough with clingfilm or a damp cloth and leave to prove for 60 minutes. The dough should appear slightly puffed up, but not doubled in size as you would expect from wheat bread dough.

♠ Preheat the oven to 200°C (400°F/Gas 6) and line a baking sheet with baking parchment. Divide the dough into 12 equal portions and roll out each portion into the shape you would like — rectangle, circle or oval. Try to roll the dough as thinly as possible, to 2 mm ($1/12$ in) if you can. You may have to work the dough in several batches. Bake the crackers for 18–20 minutes, until crisp. Once cool they should keep crisp for a few days in an airtight container.

CRUMBLY TEXTURE

Rye cracker dough can be difficult to roll and does have the tendency to break, so you may find it easier simply to roll each portion directly on the baking sheet.

FRESH FISH

When it's fresh, fish shouldn't smell 'fishy'. The eyes should have a glossy sheen and the gills will be bright red. And don't buy fish on a Monday, because it won't be the freshest catch.

SALMON TARTARE

Tartare is a finely chopped mixture of raw meat or fish with seasonings. This salmon tartare lets the quality of the fish speak for itself and the recipe delivers fresh, clean flavours in spades. Like bread, fish is best eaten super-fresh, so ask your fishmonger when it was caught, and about cheap and sustainable alternatives.

Serves 4

200 g (7 oz) raw salmon, finely diced

1 shallot, finely diced

zest and juice of 1 lemon

1 tsp finely chopped capers

1 tsp chopped dill

1 tsp snipped chives

½ tsp golden caster (superfine) sugar

½ tsp sea salt

3 tsp olive oil

♠ Put the diced salmon and the shallot into a bowl (chopping your ingredients finely will make all the difference). Add the lemon zest, capers, dill and chives and mix all the ingredients together. Season with sugar and salt. Bind all the ingredients with the olive oil and lemon juice. The acid in the lemon juice slowly cooks the salmon.

♠ Serve in a bowl with shards of rye crackers on the side.

SEE PAGE 102 FOR THE RYE CRACKERS

PUMPKIN & CHEESE SAVOURY SCROLLS

We don't always have the time to sit down and relax with a leisurely meal. Sometimes we just want food on the go. Hot or cold, on their own or alongside a hearty home-made soup, these are the perfect savoury snack.

♠ Preheat the oven to 180°C (350°F/Gas 4). Put the pumpkin cubes in a roasting tray and season with sea salt and black pepper. Sprinkle in the chopped thyme and drizzle over the olive oil and roast for 15 minutes or until tender. Set aside to cool.

♠ To make the dough, mix the flour and salt in a bowl and make a well in the centre. Crumble the yeast into the water so that it dissolves. Pour the yeasted water into the well and bring the dough together with your hands or with a spatula. As the flour is incorporated the dough will start to take shape.

♠ Turn the dough out on to a clean kitchen surface and knead for 10 minutes or until you achieve the windowpane effect (see page 29). Place in a lightly oiled bowl, cover with a damp cloth and leave to prove for about 60 minutes or until almost doubled in size.

♠ Preheat the oven to 200°C (400°F/Gas 6). Turn the dough out on to a clean surface and knock it back. Roll out the dough to a rectangle about 1 cm (½ in) thick and about 35 cm by 25 cm (14 in by 10 in). Mist the surface of the dough with water, cover with the grated cheddar and top with the roast pumpkin. Roll the dough up tightly into a cylinder. Mist the edge with water to help seal it. Cover the dough with a damp cloth and leave to prove for 20 minutes.

♠ Cut the roll into slices 4 cm (1½ in) thick and place on a baking tray, evenly spaced apart. Allow to rest for five minutes then bake for about 20 minutes. These scrolls can be served warm or cold.

CRISPY BACON FOUGASSE STICKS

Makes 35-40 strips

625 g (1 lb 6 oz / 4 ¼ cups) strong white bread flour

5 g (1 tsp) fine sea salt

5 g (1 tsp) golden caster (superfine) sugar

30 g (1 oz / 6 tsp) fresh yeast or 14 g (3 tsp) dried or fast-action yeast

310 ml (10 ¾ fl oz / 1 ¼ cups) water

200 g (7 oz) streaky bacon

a little olive oil for frying

250 g (9 oz) unsalted butter, or good-quality butcher's lard, softened

egg wash (see page 36)

This is a little piece of heaven. It's a version of fougasse, the distinctive flat, leaf-shaped bread from the south of France. This crispy bacon recipe is special to Languedoc, the French region that Duncan's family comes from.

♠ Mix together the flour, salt and sugar in a bowl and make a well in the centre. Crumble the yeast into the water and stir to dissolve, then pour the yeasted water into the well. Bring together into a dough with your hands or with a spatula.

♠ Turn the dough out on to a clean kitchen surface and knead for 10 minutes or until you achieve the windowpane effect (see page 29). Cover the bowl with a damp cloth and leave to prove for 60 minutes or until doubled in size.

♠ While the dough is proving, make the bacon butter. Fry the bacon in a dribble of oil on a low heat until the fat runs. Gradually increase the heat so you end up with little pieces of crispy bacon. Beat the bacon with the butter or lard in a bowl until evenly mixed through.

♠ Put the bacon butter on to a sheet of greaseproof paper and cover with another sheet. Roll and shape with a rolling pin to 25 cm (10 in) square and 5 mm / ¼ in thick. Put in the fridge to firm up slightly for about 30 minutes — you still want the butter to be a little soft.

♠ When the dough has proved, knock it back on a lightly floured surface. Using a rolling pin, roll and flatten it into a square large enough for the bacon butter sheet to fit on top at an angle of 45°. It should be about 40 cm (16 in) square. Place the bacon butter sheet on the dough square and fold each corner of the dough to the centre to enclose it (see opposite). Press together to seal and dust with flour.

♠ To fold the fougasse, first roll out the bacon butter dough with a rolling pin, pushing evenly away from you. Try to avoid breaking the skin of the dough as the fat will come through. Give a quarter turn and roll again to make a square of about 40 cm (16 in).

♠ Fold down the top third of the dough, then fold up the bottom third – like folding a letter to fit in an envelope. Fold in the two short sides in thirds in the same way (see top right). Flip the dough over and rest it in the fridge for 10 minutes for the butter to re-firm.

♠ Repeat the rolling and folding twice more, resting the fougasse in the fridge each time. At this stage you can freeze the dough, or keep it in the fridge for up to three days.

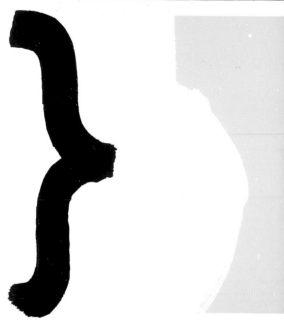

♠ Preheat the oven to 200°C (400°F/Gas 6). Roll out the fougasse on a lightly floured surface to a rectangle about 5 mm / ¼ in thick, turning it over now and again and re-flouring the surface to make sure the dough doesn't stick.

♠ Cut the fougasse into strips for your crispy bacon bites, or into the traditional leaf shape (see page 41). Place the pieces on a greased baking tray and allow to prove for 15 minutes. Wash with egg glaze and bake for 20 minutes, until risen and golden.

CALZONE BREAD PASTIES

Cornish pasty meets Italian calzone – this is our take on two classics. They may just be pizzas with a fold, but for us they are little pockets of contentment. This recipe really shows the versatility of bread, with your favourite filling enclosed within a light, soft dough. Enjoy them piping hot or tuck in while you're out and about.

Makes 4 pasties

500 g (1 lb 2 oz / 3 ⅓ cups) strong white bread flour

10 g (2 tsp) fine sea salt

5 g (1 tsp) unrefined sugar

10 g (2 tsp) fresh yeast or 7 g (1 ½ tsp) dried or fast-action yeast

270 ml (9 ½ fl oz / 1 cup plus 4 tsp) water

For the tomato sauce:

3 tsp sunflower oil

1 shallot, finely chopped

2 garlic cloves, finely chopped

1 bunch of basil, leaves picked and torn into pieces

400 g (14 oz) tin chopped tomatoes

a dash of worcestershire sauce

sea salt

♠ Mix together the flour, salt and sugar in a bowl and make a well in the centre. Crumble the yeast into the water and stir to dissolve. Pour the yeasted water into the well and bring together into a dough with your hands or with a spatula.

♠ Turn the dough out on to a clean kitchen surface and knead for 10 minutes or until you achieve the windowpane effect (see page 29). Place in a lightly oiled bowl, cover with a damp cloth and leave to prove for about 60 minutes, or until doubled in size.

♠ Turn out the dough on to a clean surface and knock it back, then divide it into four equal portions and shape into nice rounds, flattening them slightly. Either leave on the surface or put on a baking tray, cover with a damp cloth and prove for another 20 minutes.

♠ Preheat the oven to 220°C (425°F/Gas 7) and put in a pizza stone to heat up.

♠ To make the tomato sauce, warm the sunflower oil in a medium saucepan and add the shallot. Fry over a medium heat until translucent then add the garlic and basil. Warm these through before pouring in the chopped tomatoes. Cook the tomatoes down for five minutes. Finish with a dash of worcestershire sauce, season to taste with sea salt then pass through a fine sieve. Your tomato sauce is ready to go.

♠ Using a rolling pin on a floured surface roll out each circle of dough to form a round about 1 cm (½ in) and slightly smaller than a dinner plate. Spread the whole surface with tomato sauce and add your chosen toppings (see opposite) to one side. Fold the base over and pinch the edges together to seal.

♠ When ready to bake, place the calzone pasties directly on to the pizza stone and cook for about 18 minutes, until the pasties are turning golden at the edges and the filling is piping hot.

Filling 1:

Wilted spinach, sautéed mushrooms, red onion and mozzarella.

Filling 2:

Goat's cheese, pancetta and sweet onion relish (see page 53).

Filling 3:

Breakfast calzone – cooked bacon and sausage with an egg broken on top.

BUTTERS, OILS & SPREADS

Sometimes a spread of butter, a generous drizzle of good-quality oil or a dip in balsamic vinegar is all a bread needs. Infusing your oils with herbs and spices brings a whole new level of flavour and depth. At our bakery we use the leftover rind from the wheels of cheddar to make our own cheese, garlic and rosemary oil.

MAKING YOUR OWN BUTTER

There is nothing better to accompany a freshly baked loaf than lashings of butter. Why not take it a step further and make your own?

Makes 1 100 g stick

150 ml (5 fl oz)
double (heavy) cream

a clean jam jar

cold water

Bring the cream to room temperature and pour it into a jam jar; it should fill it to about a third. Screw the lid on tightly and shake vigorously. After 5–10 minutes you will feel a lump starting to form. This is the beginnings of butter, surrounded by pale buttermilk.

Shake for a couple more minutes then pour out the buttermilk (which can be used in place of milk in our Irish soda bread, see page 76). Add a little cold water to the butter, re-seal the lid and shake for a minute. Drain out the water and repeat the process until the water comes out clear. This ensures that all the buttermilk has been drained out — otherwise it would spoil the butter.

Tip the butter out on to a wooden chopping board and use butter pats (which are cheap at car-boot sales) or wooden spatulas to work it into a tight brick, ensuring you squeeze out any last remaining liquid. Raise the board at an angle so the liquid runs off.

Press into a butter mould or roll in greaseproof paper and refrigerate until needed.

FLAVOURED BUTTERS

Leave the butter to soften, then work in your flavour combos using a wooden spoon. Roll the finished butter into a log-like baton, wrap in greaseproof paper or cling film and freeze. It will keep for three months and all you need to do is cut off what you need to flavour pastas and sauces or smother on bread.

Flavourings to try:
Chopped parsley with a touch of lemon juice
Crushed garlic and sage
Chopped wild garlic leaves (see page 16)
Thyme and rock salt
Dried chilli and paprika
Crushed anchovy fillets

BUTTER & BUTTERMILK

SQUEEZE OUT THE WATER

HOME-MADE BUTTER. AMAZING!

CHOOSING OILS

From olive to rapeseed, sunflower to peanut (groundnut) and more exotic options, such as hazelnut or macadamia, the variety of oils is endless. For flavour, invest in extra virgin oils.

We now use rapeseed oil for much of our baking. It came as a bit of a revelation: we were struggling to source an affordable, high-quality olive oil and then we heard of a small producer growing and pressing rapeseed oil just a few miles down the road. It is high in healthy omega-3 oils and has a delicious, distinctive nutty flavour.

INFUSING OILS

Oils are the perfect instant accompaniment to bread, for dipping and dressings, and you can also use them to enrich your home-made bread to produce delicious treats like focaccia (see page 100).

You can either cold-infuse or hot-infuse your oils, depending on how much time you have. Cold-infusing takes longer but usually yields a tastier oil. Hot-infusing is more suited to ingredients such as cheese. At the bakery we make a delicious oil with the rinds of the cheddar cheese we use in our loaves.

To cold-infuse your oil: Simply put the herbs, spices or other ingredients into a clean, sterilised bottle and then fill with your chosen oil. Store in a cool, dark place for two to three weeks, shaking occasionally, then sieve the oil to leave it clear. To remove tiny particles, use a muslin or jelly bag sterilised by pouring boiling water through it.

To hot-infuse your oil: Put the oil and infusing ingredients in a small pan over a low heat and warm gently for five minutes. Pass the oil through a sieve to remove remnants and pouring into sterilised bottles (see page 136) for storage.

A word of warning: the decorative bottles of oil sold as gifts are treated so that the garlic cloves, herbs or other ingredients can be safely left in the bottle. When making infused oils at home it is important to strain these out at the end of the process and refrigerate the oil to help avoid developing harmful bacteria in the oil.

Flavourings to try:
Garlic and rosemary
Sage sprigs
Cracked peppercorns
Dried chilli flakes
Cheese rind and herbs

ASIAN-STYLE SPICED OIL

This is a blended rather than infused oil with a light spicy kick. Put all the ingredients in a blender and blitz together. Try spreading it on focaccia (see page 100). It can be used straight away or kept in the fridge for three days.

Makes about 100 ml (3 ½ fl oz)

90 ml (3 fl oz) rapeseed or olive oil

4 tbsp lemon juice

5 cm (2 in) piece of root ginger

3 fresh green chillies

1 tsp sea salt

1 tsp cumin seeds

1 tsp chopped fresh coriander (cilantro)

freshly ground black pepper

BALSAMIC VINEGAR

There are leagues of difference between good and bad balsamic vinegars. They range from the hugely expensive Aceto Balsamico Tradizionale di Modena (aged for over 30 years and made in tiny quantities), through Aceto Balsamico di Modena (made in the same way but not aged as long) to 'pretend' balsamic (made using red wine vinegar, a tiny bit of Aceto Balsamico and caramel to give colour). If you are buying balsamic for dipping, go for affordable but genuine Aceto Balsamico di Modena – your bread deserves it!

This is bread with serious personality. Each loaf is a genuine one-off – and sourdough just gets better and better every time you make it. This is bread as it was meant to be.

Sourdough is an ancient way of making bread but it is enjoying a real revival. It is based on natural leaven, using the wild yeasts in the air rather than commercial yeast. To make it you create a 'starter'. In the right conditions flour and water will spontaneously ferment and continue to do so if regularly 'fed'. Everything occurs at a much more natural rate, resulting in an unrivalled crust and distinctive flavour – and a loaf that is easier to digest.

Whether you're a busy stay-at-home parent, or equally busy nine-to-fiver, we'll show you how you can fit sourdough into your schedule.

MAKING YOUR SOURDOUGH STARTER

Making your starter is the first step with sourdough. It is what you will use instead of fresh or dried yeast. At The Thoughtful Bread Company, we came to call the starter 'our kid' – we had to make sure there was always someone around to look after it. Think of the starter as a living, breathing thing that requires food to keep it alive. Show it some love and your starter will give you years of bread satisfaction.

To make a sourdough loaf, you take a portion of the starter and mix it with more flour and water. You will need to begin your starter a week or two before you plan to bake with it. Starters improve with age so don't be discouraged if your first few loaves are rather bland. In time they should develop more personality.

Day 1

175 ml (5 ½ fl oz) skimmed milk

75 ml (2 ½ fl oz) live natural yoghurt

Heat the milk gently until lukewarm, place the yoghurt into a bowl and stir in the milk. (The natural yoghurt gives your starter a helping hand by introducing some friendly bacteria.)

Cover and leave at room temperature for 12–24 hours until thickened. Stir in any liquids that may have separated.

Day 2

120 g (4 ¼ oz) strong white bread flour

Stir the flour evenly into the yoghurt mixture. Cover and leave at room temperature for two days. After this time the mixture should be full of bubbles and smell pleasantly sour.

Day 4

175 g (6 oz) strong white bread flour

100 ml (3 ½ fl oz) water

40 ml (1 ¼ fl oz) milk

Add the flour to the starter and mix in the water and milk. Cover and leave again for 12–24 hours.

Day 5

The starter should be quite active and full of little bubbles. If not, give it another day or two.

Now it's time to start baking, using the recipe over the page.

TURN OVER FOR A DELICIOUS SOURDOUGH LOAF

FEEDING YOUR STARTER

Like any living being, your starter needs feeding. The best time to do this is right after you have made some bread. You simply want to bulk up what is left of the starter back to what you originally had.

To the remaining starter add:

300 g (10 ½ oz / 2 cups) strong white bread flour

300 ml (10 ½ fl oz) water

Add the flour and water to your remaining starter and mix vigorously until combined. Set aside for at least 12–24 hours for it to feed on the fresh flour and water before you remove any more starter to bake with.

At our bakery we use and feed our starter every day, but if you don't intend baking for some time you can refrigerate the starter for up to five days in an airtight plastic container before it needs feeding again. Remove from the fridge two hours before you intend using it.

Your sourdough starter can also be frozen and then defrosted 48 hours before it's needed again. Or else dry it in the oven at a low temperature – around 120°C (235°F/Gas ½). When it is dry, crumble it and store in an airtight container such as a kilner jar. You can rehydrate it by feeding it as normal.

If you ever see a thin layer of watery or vinegary liquid forming on the surface, this is your starter telling you it's very hungry. Pour off the liquid and feed it straightaway, or risk having to begin all over again!

KEEP IT GOING

Never use up all your starter - always keep a small amount so that you have something to feed.

If your starter is stored at room temperature, feed it daily. If your starter is stored in the fridge, feed it every four to five days.

WHITE SOURDOUGH LOAF

Makes 2 small 400 g or 1 lb loaves

500 g (1 lb 2 oz / 3 ⅓ cups)
strong white bread flour

400 g (14 oz / 1½ cups) sourdough starter

250 ml (9 fl oz / 1 cup) water

15 g (3 tsp) fine sea salt

5 g (1 tsp) unrefined sugar

When your starter is alive and kicking, it's time to get baking. For these rustic loaves we suggest you prove them for the second time in a suitably sized bowl lined with a couche cloth, or else make simple cob or pouch loaves (see page 40). If you're feeling adventurous, try the stunning couronne bordelaise shown in the pictures opposite.

Mix together the flour, starter and water in a bowl and add the salt and sugar. Turn out on to a clean kitchen surface and knead for 10 minutes or until you achieve the windowpane effect (see page 29). Put the dough in a lightly oiled bowl, cover with a damp cloth and leave to prove for 2½–3 hours. It will rise, but not anywhere near as much as with a yeasted bread.

Turn the dough out on to a clean surface and knock it back. Shape into two loaves. Flour generously and place each loaf seam-side up in bowl lined with a well-floured couche cloth – a floured tea towel will also work fine. Leave to prove for 2½–3 hours or until risen by half.

Preheat the oven to 220°C (425°F/Gas 7) and place a roasting tray in the bottom. Turn the loaves out on to a baking tray or hot baking stone. Flour, score or glaze (see page 36), put in the oven, and steam by adding ice cubes or cold water to the roasting tray. Bake for 35–40 minutes, or until a good crust has formed.

FITTING SOURDOUGH BAKING AROUND A BUSY SCHEDULE

The biggest challenge with sourdough is finding the time to bake it, so here are two ways to fit it into your day.

Daytime proving for at-home parents

1. Mix and knead your dough first thing in the morning, then put aside to prove while you take the children to school.

2. After 2½–3 hours – in the mid-morning – turn out the dough, portion and shape it.

3. You now have plenty of time for the loaves to prove. They will need 2½–3 hours.

4. Bake your sourdough after lunch and it will be cooling while you do the school run.

Overnight proving for nine-to-fivers

1. Mix and knead your dough when you get home from work. You now have a few hours to get dinner on, sit back and relax.

2. Shape the bread and put it into proving bowls just before bedtime. Now refrigerate the loaves for around eight hours. If you can, set your oven to start preheating about 30 minutes before you get up.

3. First thing in the morning, take out your loaves – they will need an hour before they are ready for baking. Preheat your oven, have breakfast, then put your loaf on to bake. You now have 40 minutes to shower and change before taking your sourdough out of the oven and putting it on a cooling rack to enjoy when you get home. Better still, wrap it in paper and bring it to work to share.

WRAP THE DOUGH BALLS

COURONNE BORDELAISE

Having mastered the wizardry of savoury bread-making, it's time to turn your attentions to these little sweet morsels to give and share.

This next step as you travel the road of real bread is all about embracing everything that's sugar-coated, cinnamon-scented, fruity or downright chocolatey. Whether for the breakfast table or afternoon tea, these buns, loaves and swirls are packed with butter, milk and eggs to give a richer, softer dough.

It's about time we got those endorphins pumping, because we all deserve a little indulgence in our lives!

RICH BRIOCHE LOAVES

Brioche is a French bread enriched with eggs and butter. It is sometimes broken down into three types: poor man's, middle class and rich man's brioche, depending on the ingredients. Rich, velvety and almost flaky, this recipe is most definitely rich man's brioche – and why not: we can all live like kings every now and again.

Makes 2 small 400 g or 1 lb loaves

500 g (1 lb 2 oz / 3⅓ cups) strong white bread flour

5 g (1 tsp) fine sea salt

20 g (4 tsp) golden caster (superfine) sugar

15 g (3 tsp) fresh yeast or 10 g (2 tsp) dried or fast-action yeast

50 ml (1¾ fl oz) water

6 eggs

300 g (10 ½ oz) unsalted butter, softened

egg wash (see page 36)

♠ This is the one of the few recipes where we recommend using a mixer – otherwise the kneading time is quite long and intensive. Combine the flour, salt and sugar in the mixer bowl. Crumble the yeast into the water, stir to dissolve and add to the flour. Using the dough hook, start the mixer on a slow speed and add the eggs one by one. The mix will appear quite wet but that is exactly what we are looking for. Continue mixing on a medium speed until the dough just starts to come away from the sides. This can take up to 10 minutes or more.

♠ Dice the butter and add it a third at a time while continuing to mix. Add the next third only once the first is fully incorporated. Continue mixing until the dough comes away cleanly from the sides. It will still be fairly wet but should now be smooth and elastic.

♠ Place the dough in a lightly oiled bowl and cover with a damp cloth. Allow to prove for 60 minutes at room temperature, then transfer to the fridge and leave for several hours or even overnight. This will firm it up and make it easier to handle and shape.

♠ When ready to make your brioches, remove the dough from the fridge. (You could use part of this recipe amount and return the remainder to the fridge – it will keep well for two to three days.) Portion the dough into thirds on a floured kitchen surface and grease and flour two baking tins. Shape the dough as for a tin loaf (see page 28) and put in the tins. Cover with a damp cloth and leave to prove for about two hours or until well risen but not quite doubled.

♠ Preheat the oven to 200°C (400°F/Gas 6) and put a roasting tray in the bottom. Brush the brioche loaves with egg wash, then place in the oven and steam by adding ice cubes or cold water to the tray. Cook for 10 minutes then reduce the temperature to 180°C (350°F/Gas 4) and cook for a further 25–30 minutes, until golden on top.

CHOCOLATE BRIOCHE BUNS

To the recipe on the left add 100 g (3½ oz / ⅔ cup) dark chocolate chips – keeping some aside to garnish the buns – to the mixed dough. Mix until evenly distributed.

When you take the dough out of the fridge, divide it into 16 buns. Line a muffin tray with muffin cases or baking parchment, filling each with a brioche roll. Cover with a damp cloth and allow to prove for about two hours or until well risen but not quite doubled.

When ready to bake, brush each bun with egg wash and add a few pieces of chopped chocolate. Bake for 10 minutes at 200°C (400°F/Gas 6), reduce to 180°C (350°F/Gas 4) and cook for a further 8–10 minutes.

CINNAMON SWIRLS

For the lovers of cinnamon out there, this one is for you – a rich, soft dough bursting with cinnamon and brown sugar. Nothing can compare to the smell of these wonderful sweet treats as they bake – what a way to wake up in the morning. And all the work can be done the night before. Make the dough, roll it, shape it and simply leave it covered in the fridge until you are ready to cook.

Makes 12 swirls

900 g (2 lb / 6 cups) strong white bread flour

10 g (2 tsp) fine sea salt

100 g (3 ½ oz / ½ cup) golden caster (superfine) sugar

100 g (3 ½ oz) unsalted butter, softened

20 g (4 tsp) fresh yeast or 14 g (3 tsp) dried or fast-action yeast

180 ml (6 fl oz / ¾ cup) water

280 ml (9 ½ fl oz) milk

2 eggs

250 g (9 oz / 1 ¼ cups) soft brown sugar

25 g (1 oz / 10 tsp) ground cinnamon

egg wash (see page 36)

sugar glaze (see page 36)

For the sugared raisin filling:

150 g (5 ½ oz) soft brown sugar

100 g (3 ½ oz / ⅔ cup) plain (all-purpose) white flour

100 g (3 ½ oz) unsalted butter, cut into cubes

100 g (3 ½ oz) raisins

icing sugar glaze (see page 36)

♠ Combine the flour, salt and sugar in a bowl. Dice the butter and rub it in with your fingertips until the mixture resembles breadcrumbs. Make a well in the centre. Crumble the yeast into the water, stir to dissolve and pour the yeasted water and milk into the well. Add the eggs and bring together into a dough with your hands or a spatula. This is a soft, supple dough and may feel a little wet to begin with.

♠ Turn it out on to a clean kitchen surface and knead for 10 minutes or until you achieve the windowpane effect (see page 29). Put the dough in a lightly oiled bowl, cover with a damp cloth and prove for about 60 minutes at room temperature. Then put it in the fridge for at least 30 minutes, until it firms slightly. This will help when you roll it out.

♠ Turn the dough out on to a lightly floured surface and knock it back. Roll it out with a rolling pin to make a rectangle about 1 cm (½ in) thick and measuring about 42 cm by 30 cm (17 in by 12 in).

♠ Mix the brown sugar and cinnamon. Mist the surface of the dough with water from a spray bottle and dust generously with the cinnamon sugar mixture. Mist again and roll up the dough into a tight cylinder, misting the seam to make sure it sticks. Cut the roll into 12 slices, each a little over 2.5cm (1 in) thick. Place the rolls, well spaced apart, on a baking tray lined with baking parchment. Either cover with a damp cloth and allow to prove for 60 minutes or cover with clingfilm and place in the fridge until morning. (If refrigerating, take the swirls out 90 minutes before you want to bake them.)

♠ Preheat the oven to 190°C (375°F/Gas 5). Before baking brush each swirl with egg wash. Bake for 15 minutes, until lightly golden. Place on a wire cooling rack and brush with sugar glaze while still warm.

SUGARED RAISIN ROLLS

For an alternative filling, combine the brown sugar and flour and rub in the butter with your fingertips until the texture is nice and crumbly. Mist the rolled dough, spread the sugar and flour mixture across the rectangle and top with raisins. Roll up the dough and portion, then continue as for the cinnamon swirls. Once cooked, place on a wire rack and when cool drizzle with the icing sugar glaze.

NIBBED SUGAR

These large, hard sugar crystals are also called pearl or hail sugar and are popular in Scandinavian baking. If you can't find it easily, improvise by smashing a couple of sugar cubes into small pieces.

BATH BUNS

500 g (1 lb 2 oz / 3 ⅓ cups)
strong white bread flour

75 g (2 ½ oz / ⅓ cup) golden caster
(superfine) sugar

5 g (1 tsp) fine sea salt

15 g (3 tsp) fresh yeast or 10 g (2 tsp)
dried or fast-action yeast

275 ml (9½ fl oz / 1 cup plus 1 tbsp) milk

1 egg

zest of 1 lemon

zest of ½ orange

75 g (2 ½ oz) unsalted butter,
softened

10 sugar cubes

egg wash (see page 36)

milk glaze (see page 36)

nibbed (pearl) sugar and a handful
of raisins to garnish

The Bath bun is a sweet, yeasted bun baked with a sugar cube in its centre and covered in nibbed sugar once out of the oven. This recipe is our tribute to the city of Bath – the place where The Thoughtful Bread Company's life began – and our own citrussy riff on the original.

♠ This is one of the few occasions when we recommend that you use a mixer, as this recipe requires extensive kneading. It is not a necessity and if you think you have the stamina for it by all means go for it by hand, but the assistance of a mixer will greatly speed up the process.

♠ Combine the flour, sugar and salt in the mixer bowl. Crumble the yeast into the milk, stir to dissolve and add the yeasted milk, egg and citrus zest to the flour mixture. Using the dough hook, knead the dough on a medium speed. Initially it will appear quite wet. Continue mixing until the dough starts to come away from the sides.

♠ Dice the butter, drop it in and carry on mixing until all the butter is incorporated. The dough should be soft, supple and silky. Transfer to a lightly oiled bowl, cover with a damp cloth and leave to prove for 90 minutes or until doubled in size.

♠ Turn out the dough on to a lightly floured work surface, knock back and divide into 10 equal amounts. Roll each portion into a small ball, place seam-side up on the kitchen surface and push a sugar cube into each roll. Turn the balls over and roll gently for a second time – just enough to trap the sugar cube within.

♠ Place the buns on a baking tray lined with parchment, leaving enough room so that they won't touch as they expand. Cover with a damp cloth and leave to prove for 90 minutes or until almost doubled in size.

♠ Preheat the oven to 190°C (375°F/Gas 5). Brush each bun with egg wash and bake for 15–18 minutes, until evenly golden. Transfer to a wire rack to cool. While warm, brush each bun with milk glaze and top with a mixture of nibbed sugar and raisins.

HOT CROSS BUNS

Hot cross buns are synonymous with Easter, but if you ask us they are something to be enjoyed all year round – warm from the oven, toasted and smothered with butter or simply with a cup of tea. The secret to this recipe is our all-purpose mincemeat – boozy soaked fruit with that nice balance of spice.

Makes 10 buns

500 g (1 lb 2 oz / 3 ⅓ cups) strong white bread flour

5 g (1 tsp) fine sea salt

50 g (1 ¾ oz / ¼ cup) golden caster (superfine) sugar

75 g (2 ½ oz) unsalted butter, softened

15 g (3 tsp) fresh yeast or 10 g (2 tsp) dried or fast-action yeast

90 ml (3 fl oz) water

150 ml (5 fl oz / a scant ⅔ cup) milk

1 egg

175 g (6 oz) mincemeat (see page 132)

For the paste:

100 g (3 ½ oz / ⅔ cup) plain (all-purpose) white flour

30 g (1 oz) golden caster (superfine) sugar

80 ml (2 ½ fl oz / ⅓ cup) milk

♣ Mix together the flour, salt and sugar in a bowl. Dice the butter and rub it in with your fingertips. Make a well in the flour mixture.

♣ Crumble the yeast into the water so that it dissolves and pour the yeasted water, milk and egg into the well. Bring the dough together with your hands or with a spatula. This is quite a soft dough and may feel a little wet and sticky, but don't panic, just be persistent.

♣ Turn the dough out on to a clean kitchen surface and knead for 10 minutes. Just as you reach the windowpane stage (see page 29), gently knead in the mincemeat so the fruit is evenly distributed without getting all broken up. Put the dough in a lightly oiled bowl, cover with a damp cloth and leave to prove for about 80–90 minutes or until doubled in size.

♣ After proving, cut the dough into 10 equal pieces, form into rolls and place on a non-stick baking tray or a tray lined with baking parchment, leaving enough room in between each so that the buns can prove and grow without touching. Leave to prove again for 60–80 minutes or until doubled in size.

♣ Preheat the oven to 190°C (375°F/Gas 5), then make up the paste for the crosses. Mix the flour, sugar and milk in a bowl – the paste needs to be the consistency of thick custard. Brush the buns with beaten egg yolk, spoon the paste into a piping bag with a 3 mm (⅛ in) nozzle and pipe a cross on each one. Bake the buns for 16–18 minutes, until rich gold in colour. Transfer to a wire rack to cool.

TURN OVER FOR OUR SECRET MINCEMEAT RECIPE

GLOSSY GLAZE

For a wonderful shine and finger-licking stickiness, brush the cooked buns with simple sugar glaze while still warm. See page 36 for the recipe.

See page 36 for the recipe.

UNCLE PAUL'S MINCEMEAT
(& OUR FRUIT LOAF)

Makes about 2 kg (4 lb 8 oz)

500 g (1 lb 2 oz / 3 cups) sultanas

500 g (1 lb 2 oz / 3 cups) raisins

250 g (9 oz / 1¾ cups) currants

zest and juice of 3 oranges

zest and juice of 2 lemons

250 g (9 oz) soft brown sugar

250 g (9 oz)
unsalted butter, melted

5 g (2 tsp) ground nutmeg

5 g (1 tsp) ground cinnamon

2.5 g (1 tsp) ground cloves

175 ml (6 fl oz) dark rum

175 ml (6 fl oz) brandy

This recipe was given to me by my Uncle Paul and it is a winner. The first time Duncan tried it he wasn't sure whether to eat it or drink it because of the amount of alcohol. We use this mincemeat all year round – for mince pies and hot cross buns, raisin swirls and our fruit loaf.

♠ Combine all the ingredients in a large mixing bowl. Stir well, transfer to sterilised jars (see page 136) and store in the fridge. Leave to marinate for at least six weeks to let the flavours develop. This mincemeat will keep for at least a year in the fridge.

FRUIT LOAF

Makes 2 small 400 g or 1 lb loaves

500 g (1 lb 2 oz / 3⅓ cups) strong white bread flour

10 g (2 tsp) fine sea salt

20 g (4 tsp) golden caster (superfine) sugar

50 g (1¾ oz) unsalted butter, softened

10g (2 tsp) fresh yeast or 7 g (1½ tsp) dried or fast-action yeast

300 ml (10½ fl oz) milk

1 egg

100 g (3½ oz) mincemeat

egg wash (see page 36)

♠ Mix together the flour, salt and sugar in a bowl. Dice the butter and rub it in with your fingertips and make a well in the centre.

♠ Crumble the yeast into the milk, stir to dissolve and pour the yeasted milk and the egg into the well. Bring together into a dough with your hands or with a spatula.

♠ Turn the dough out on to a clean kitchen surface and knead for 10 minutes. Just as you reach the windowpane stage (see page 29), gently knead in the mincemeat. Put the dough in a lightly oiled bowl, cover with a damp cloth and leave to prove for 80–90 minutes or until almost doubled.

♠ Cut the dough in half and shape as two balls (see page 40) or two tin loaves (see page 28). Place in two lightly oiled 400 g or 1 lb loaf tins or well spaced on a baking tray lined with baking parchment and leave to prove again for 60–80 minutes or until doubled in size.

♠ Preheat the oven to 190°C (375°F/Gas 5). Brush each loaf with egg wash and place in the oven. Bake for 35 minutes, rotating the loaves if necessary to ensure they turn an even golden brown colour. (The alcohol in the mincemeat all cooks off during the baking.)

SUMMER JAM (OR CUSTARD) DOUGHNUTS

With this recipe you will be making the freshest doughnuts you have ever tasted. All soft and light and waiting to be enjoyed.

♠ Combine the flour, salt and sugar in a bowl. Dice the butter and rub it in with your fingertips until the mixture resembles fine breadcrumbs. Make a well in the centre. Crumble the yeast into the water, stir to dissolve and pour the yeasted water into the well, along with the milk and eggs. Bring together into a dough with your hands or with a spatula. This is quite a soft, supple dough so if things start to get a little messy just keep going — it will most likely come out fine.

♠ Turn the dough out on to a clean kitchen surface and knead for 10 minutes or until you achieve the windowpane effect (see page 20). Put the dough in a lightly oiled bowl, cover with a damp cloth and leave to prove for about 40 minutes at room temperature or until almost doubled in size. Then transfer it to the fridge for 20 minutes to allow it to firm up slightly.

♠ Turn the dough out on to a clean surface and knock it back. Cut into 13 equal pieces, form into balls and place on a tray lined with baking parchment. Leave to prove again for 40 minutes — you don't want your dough to prove too much, as you still need to be able to handle it.

♠ A thermostatically controlled deep-fat fryer is the best thing to use for cooking your doughnuts; you could use a deep saucepan, but be extremely careful to fill it only a third of the way up with vegetable oil and not to overheat it. Preheat the oil to 170°C (340°F). Using a slotted spoon, transfer the doughnuts to the oil, cooking in small batches. Make sure to leave enough room as they will expand during cooking. Fry for three minutes on each side or until golden brown.

♠ Transfer to kitchen paper to absorb any excess oil. To fill, make a small hole in the side of the doughnut with a skewer. Use a piping bag fitted with a 3 mm (⅛ in) nozzle to fill each one with your favourite jam. Then while the doughnuts are still warm, dust and roll them in caster sugar, mixed with the cinnamon if you like.

CUSTARD FILLING

If you are not a fan of jam why not try a few custard-filled doughnuts? Make a thick custard and simply pipe it in as you would the jam.

WHY NOT TRY...

Plum jam: 1.5 kg (3 lb 5 oz) plums, 1.5 kg (3 lb 5 oz/7 cups) sugar.

Rhubarb & ginger jam: 1.5 kg (3 lb 5 oz) rhubarb, 1.5 kg (3 lb 5 oz/ 7 cups) sugar, 60 g (2 oz/4 tbsp) grated root ginger.

Peach & cardamom jam: 1 kg (2 lb 4 oz) peaches, 1 kg (2 lb 4 oz/5 cups) sugar, juice of 1 lemon, 2 tsp crushed cardamom pods.

OUR JAM-MAKING TIPS

→ Choose fruit that is decent quality. Get rid of anything past its best and make the jam as soon as you can.

→ Jam works off a simple basic ratio — half sugar to half fruit. Fully dissolve the sugar over a gentle heat before bringing the fruit and sugar mixture slowly to boiling point, then boil briskly.

→ How long a jam needs to boil depends on the amount of sugar and moisture in the fruit.

→ Always use an enamelled saucepan or stainless steel preserving pan and a wooden spoon, as cast iron will flavour the jam.

→ To test if jam has reached setting point, put a little on a plate. If it sets in a minute or two it is done.

→ Always used sterilised jars, or your jam will spoil. Wash in warm, soapy water, rinse and place in an oven at 180°C (350°F/Gas 4) for 10 minutes. Fill while still warm.

SUMMER BERRY JAM

Makes 4-5 jars

500 g (1 lb 2 oz / 3⅓ cups) strawberries

500 g (1 lb 2 oz / 4 cups) raspberries

500 g (1 lb 2 oz / 4 cups) redcurrants

125 ml (4 fl oz / ½ cup) water

1.5 kg (3 lb 5 oz / 7 cups) caster (superfine) sugar

Home-made jam tastes so much better than anything shop bought, and every summer there's a glut of produce just calling out to be preserved so that it can delight all year long. We've given a few tips that will help you convert a wide array of fruits into an abundance of jam-packed jars.

★ Pick over the fruit and rinse it briefly. Add the fruit, water and sugar to a preserving pan and stir over a gentle heat until the sugar has dissolved. Turn up the heat to medium and continue stirring until the mixture reaches boiling point. Boil steadily for 30 minutes, skimming off any scum that comes to the surface. Test the jam to see if it has reached setting point (see opposite). When ready, pour it into sterilised jars (see opposite) and seal while still warm.

BANANA BREAD

Makes 2 small 400 g or 1 lb loaves

225 g (8 oz / 1½ cups) plain white flour

5 g (1 tsp) fine sea salt

1 heaped tsp baking powder

1 tsp ground cinnamon

110 g (3¾ oz / ½ cup) golden caster (superfine) sugar

75 ml (2½ fl oz / ⅓ cup) milk

75 g (2½ oz) unsalted butter, melted

1 egg

a few drops of vanilla extract

65 g (2¼ oz / ½ cup) chopped pecan nuts (walnuts are a great alternative)

4 medium-sized ripe bananas, mashed

The secret to banana bread is well-ripened bananas. Bright yellow, firm bananas – stay away from them! The black bananas with a few blemishes – the ones that most people turn their noses up at – are what you want. They are packed with flavour and beautifully sweet. This is a 'quick bread' that doesn't use any yeast.

♠ Preheat the oven to 190°C (375°F/Gas 5). Mix the flour, salt, baking powder, cinnamon and sugar in a bowl. Add the milk, melted butter, egg and vanilla extract and combine. Fold in the pecans or walnuts and the mashed bananas.

♠ Grease two 400 g or 1 lb loaf tins with a little butter, then dust with flour, tipping out the excess. Divide the mixture between the two tins and bake for 45 minutes. The bread is cooked when the tip of a knife pushed into the centre comes out clean. Remove the loaves from the tins and place on a wire rack to cool.

♠ Try the loaf for breakfast, mid-afternoon or even warmed through with a scoop of ice cream as a dessert. An all-round winner.

STICKY LOAVES

If you ever find that a loaf has stuck to a baking tin and simply refuses to come out, take a wet cloth, sit the tin on top and leave for several minutes. Like magic the loaf should simply pop out.

DARK & WHITE CHOCOLATE MINI MUFFINS

Makes 12 full-size or 30 mini muffins

225 g (8 oz / 1½ cups) plain (all-purpose) white flour

10 g (2 tsp) baking powder

½ tsp fine sea salt

50 g (1¾ oz / ⅓ cup) dark chocolate chips

50 g (1¾ oz / ⅓ cup) white chocolate chips

125 g (4½ oz) natural yoghurt

125 ml (4 fl oz / ½ cup) milk

1 egg

75 g (2½ oz) unsalted butter, melted and cooled

a drop of vanilla extract

When those sweet cravings kick in and the cupboard is bare, the time has come to make your own sweet little muffins. Ready in minutes, these are bite-sized indulgences. You can adapt the basic recipe – swap the chocolate chips for the same weight of blueberries or raspberries, or add raisins and replace the vanilla with 1 tsp of cinnamon.

♠ Preheat the oven to 180°C (350°F/Gas 4). Sift the flour, baking powder and salt into a bowl and stir in the chocolate chips, reserving a few to top each muffin. In a separate bowl whisk the yoghurt, milk, egg and melted butter, then add the vanilla extract. Fold the yoghurt mixture into the flour and chocolate.

♠ Don't over-mix: fold just enough to incorporate the flour. You want to retain the rough, broken texture of a muffin — too smooth and you will find yourself making a sponge.

♠ Line a muffin tray or mini muffin tray with cases. For full-size muffins, three-quarters fill with the muffin mix; for the mini muffins use a heaped teaspoonful for each one. Top with a few chocolate chips. Bake for 16 minutes, until well risen and springy to the touch.

SILICONE MOULDS

Back at our bakery we offer bite-size mini muffins - great for when school groups visit. We use silicone moulds, available in kitchen shops. You can freeze them, microwave them, put them in the oven and re-use them over and over... they really are fantastic and worth the investment.

The Bread Revolution is about crust-to-crust eating – making, using and savouring every morsel of your fantastic loaves. You've trusted us to show you how to get into baking real bread at home, and our promise now is to give you some ways of using all the versatility of bread to make sure nothing goes to waste.

As we near the end of our bread-making journey (at least for now...), here are some crafty and really rather thrifty ways to ensure every single last crumb of your hard work is enjoyed.

From summery salads to heart-warming desserts and cheeky booze-fuelled shots, this section has it all. And what's more, it's all about saving you some rather serious cash as well. Get stuck in.

PANZANELLA SALAD
WITH FORAGED LEAVES

100 ml (3½ fl oz) olive oil

2 tbsp balsamic vinegar

4 thick slices of stale bread

500 g (1 lb 2 oz) tomatoes,
a selection of different types,
roughly chopped into bite-size pieces

1 red onion, finely sliced

a small bunch of basil

a handful of seasonal foraged leaves,
or a mix of salad leaves

sea salt &
freshly ground black pepper

This is a classic Italian salad that transforms chunks of stale-ish bread with the juice of sweet tomatoes and a rich dressing of balsamic vinegar and olive oil. A handful of readily available foraged leaves gives this dish a real lift.

♣ Combine the oil and vinegar in a jam jar or small bowl and season the dressing to taste. Tear the bread into pieces roughly the same size as the chopped tomatoes and put in a large bowl with the tomatoes, onion and dressing. Mix so that everything is mingled together then leave to sit for about an hour at room temperature for the flavours to blend and the bread to soak up the juices.

♣ Just before serving, check the seasoning, then tear up the basil, wash and dry the foraged or salad leaves, and add these to the salad. Give it a good stir and serve.

DUNCAN'S FORAGED LEAVES

For this recipe, Duncan braved the hedgerows and fields near the bakery to collect a range of leaves that can be found in early summer. He used Jack-by-the-hedge, chickweed, wild sorrel, ox-eye daisy and young dandelion leaves (see page 16 for more about foraging).

BLOODY MARY

GAZPACHO SHOTS

Serves 6

3 plum tomatoes

1 red (bell) pepper

1 red chilli

1 shallot

½ cucumber

1 garlic clove

1 litre (35 fl oz / 4 cups) tomato juice

a dash of balsamic vinegar

a dash of worcestershire sauce

a small bunch of basil, leaves picked

100 g (3½ oz) slightly stale bread

sea salt & freshly ground black pepper

vodka to serve

On a warm summer evening, this is the ideal cold aperitif. Make it with the ripest, juiciest tomatoes you can find, and serve it with chilli and a small dash of chilled vodka for a refreshing kick.

♠ Roughly chop the tomatoes and vegetables and put them in a liquidiser with the garlic, tomato juice, balsamic vinegar, worcestershire sauce and basil leaves. Blend until smooth and season lightly.

♠ Soak the bread in water for a few minutes, then squeeze out the excess and add the bread to the liquidiser. Blend again and season to taste.

♠ Put in the refrigerator to chill for at least an hour, and chill the vodka. To serve, put a little vodka in a shot glass, and fill up with the gazpacho.

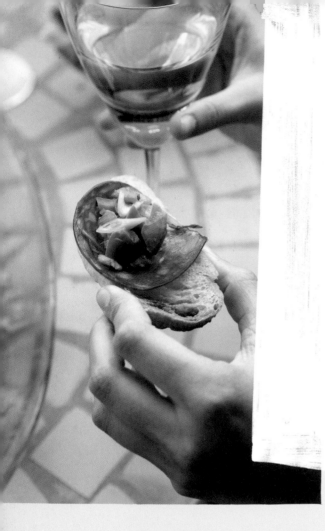

SLÁINTE

KINGSTON

LUCKY GUY

BRUSCHETTA & CROSTINI

Like two good friends, bruschetta and crostini have loads in common but distinctive personalities. A bit like the two of us. Bruschetta is toasted bread rubbed with garlic and drizzled with oil – so that's Duncan, with his French roots. Crostini are simply grilled – more Patrick's style. Both are crunchy, light and utterly delicious.

Serves 4

16 slices of slightly stale baguette

olive oil

2 garlic cloves, peeled and halved

sea salt & freshly ground black pepper

♠ First make the toppings (see opposite). For the guacamole, mash the avocado flesh in a bowl with a fork, then add the onion, crushed garlic and lime juice. Season with sea salt.

♠ For the tomato salsa, mix the tomatoes and basil in a bowl. Season with olive oil, a pinch of sea salt and some ground black pepper.

♠ For the chorizo and pepper topping, mix the pepper and chilli with a dash of olive oil and a pinch of sea salt. Top each slice of chorizo with a little of the pepper mixture.

♠ For the cream cheese and chive topping, simply mix the cream cheese with the chives and season to taste.

♠ Drizzle each slice of bread with olive oil, then rub half of the bread slices with garlic. Place under the grill (broiler) to toast, then spoon on the toppings.

OTHER GREAT TOPPINGS

Why not try… mozzarella and chilli, fig and goat's cheese, roast beef and horseradish, smoked salmon and dill, wild garlic pesto (see page 91), prosciutto and melon, sautéed mushroom, your favourite cheese and chutney (see page 57), olive tapenade and feta.

Guacamole topping:

1 avocado, peeled and stoned
½ red onion, finely chopped
½ garlic clove, crushed
juice of 1 lime

Tomato salsa topping:

2 tomatoes, roughly chopped
a small bunch of fresh basil,
leaves shredded

Chorizo & pepper topping:

1 green pepper, finely chopped
½ red chilli, finely chopped
4 slices of chorizo

Cream cheese & chive topping:

50 g (1¾ oz / ¼ cup) cream cheese
1 tsp snipped chives

CARAMEL PAIN PERDU

2 thick-cut slices of brioche
(see page 124) or white bread,
crusts removed

50 g (1¾ oz) golden caster (superfine)
sugar, plus 2 tbsp for the caramel

50 ml (1¾ fl oz) milk

a drop of vanilla extract

1 egg

a knob of unsalted butter

vanilla ice cream to serve

Pain perdu literally means 'lost bread'. It is just like French toast – dipped in a mixture of egg and milk and then fried in butter. This version is fried in caramel instead, making an amazing dessert – one of Patrick's favourites. Much more than the sum of its parts, you would never think you are just eating bread and ice cream. But believe us, it's good! Sweet, moist, but with a crunchy coating.

♠ Cut each brioche or bread slice into two, then whisk together the sugar (reserving the 2 tbsp for the caramel), milk, vanilla and egg.

♠ Warm a dry heavy-based pan on a medium heat and add 2 tbsp of sugar. Allow the sugar to melt and caramelise to a light golden colour, then carefully add the butter and stir in.

♠ Soak each piece of bread in the egg mix and add to the caramelised sugar. Cook until golden on all sides. Serve warm with a scoop of vanilla ice cream.

HEART-WARMING BREAD & BUTTER PUDDING
(WITH FRUIT COMPOTE)

Serves 6

8–10 slices of slightly stale brioche (see page 124) or white bread

50 g (1¾ oz / ¼ cup) unsalted butter

50 g (1¾ oz) blueberries, blackberries or redcurrants

250 ml (9 fl oz / 1 cup) milk

50 ml (1¾ fl oz) single (pouring) cream

3 eggs

50 g (1¾ oz / ¼ cup) golden caster (superfine) sugar

½ tsp ground cinnamon

½ tsp ground nutmeg

3 tbsp marmalade (optional)

For the berry compote:

100 g (3½ oz / ¾ cup) berries – blackberries are ideal

3 tsp golden caster (superfine) sugar

zest of 1 lime

a handful of mint leaves, chopped

Bread and butter pudding is one of those comfort foods that can't help but make you feel warm on the inside. In this recipe we have added some summer berries for a touch of freshness and lightness. You can also give the pudding a glaze of marmalade for a pleasingly bittersweet note. We suggest serving this dessert with a sharp fruit compote, which really cuts through the sweetness.

♠ Butter each slice of bread and cut in half. (Using brioche adds that extra level of richness to the final dessert, but any good-quality white bread will work just fine.) Brush an ovenproof dish with melted butter then line the base of the dish with overlapping slices of buttered bread. Spread the berries over the initial bread layer and cover with a second layer of overlapping bread slices.

♠ Preheat the oven to 170°C (325°F/Gas 3). Whisk together the milk, cream, eggs, sugar and spices. Pour the mixture over the bread slices and leave to stand for 20 minutes, then put in the oven and bake for 30 minutes, until rich and golden on top.

♠ As the pudding cooks, prepare the compote. Put the berries and sugar in a pan on a medium heat and cook gently for a few minutes, until the fruit softens. Stir in the lime zest and chopped mint. Adjust the sweetness to taste — ideally you want the compote to have a little sharpness.

♠ Warm the marmalade gently, if using, and thin it out slightly with a little water if needed. Remove the pudding from the oven and brush the top with the marmalade to create a bittersweet glaze. Whether glazing or not, replace in the oven and cook for a further 10 minutes. Serve warm with the compote.

FORAGED FRUIT

Blackberries are freely available and easily foraged – Duncan is forever bringing back hoards of fresh berries. You could also try strawberries, raspberries, gooseberries, blueberries or even plums. Simply adjust the amount of sugar to the sweetness of the fruit. A little mint, lemon or lime gives a refreshing lift.

- SUMMER - PUDDING

The secret to a fantastic summer pudding is the quality of the bread. While it is a great way to use up a loaf that is a couple of days old, pre-sliced mass-produced 'bread' simply won't cut it. The pudding won't hold together and your efforts deserve better. But now that you are making your own real bread that won't be an issue.

Serves 6

a little melted butter, to grease the bowl

6–8 slices of white bread

300 g (10 ½ oz / 2 ½ cups) raspberries

150 g (5 ½ oz / 1 ¼ cups) blackberries

150 g (5 ½ oz / 1 ¼ cups) redcurrants

50 g (1 ¾ oz / ¼ cup) golden caster (superfine) sugar

1 tsp finely chopped mint

single (pouring) cream to serve

♠ Prepare a 500 ml (17 fl oz) pudding basin by brushing the inside with melted butter — a deep breakfast bowl also works well. Line the bowl with clingfilm, leaving enough overhang to cover the top of the pudding. This will help when it comes to unmoulding.

♠ Remove the crusts from the bread, then cut a circle that will fit the top of the basin and keep it aside. Line the pudding basin with overlapping bread slices, making sure there are no gaps.

♠ Put the berries and sugar in a saucepan on a medium heat and cook down gently for a couple of minutes, until the fruits have softened and the juices have run. Stir in the chopped mint.

♠ Fill the lined pudding basin with the fruit, holding back some of the juices for later. Cover with a final slice of bread and fold the clingfilm over to seal.

♠ Place a saucer or small plate on top, making sure it fits inside the bowl. Press it down and put a heavy weight on the saucer. Leave it in the fridge overnight, or for a whole day if you can.

♠ If you have a chance, take a peek at the pudding before you come to serve it, to check that the juices have soaked through. If there are white areas, carefully pour in some of the reserved juices, letting them run down inside the clingfilm to moisten the bread.

♠ To serve, unwrap the clingfilm from the top, turn out on to a plate and then remove the rest of the clingfilm. Fantastic served with pouring cream.

ALL-YEAR BERRIES

The berry mixture we've suggested allows for a lovely balance of colour as well as sweetness, but you could add blackcurrants or strawberries instead - it's best to keep it to three types of fruit, and include raspberries as one of them. Ideally fresh berries work best, but you can also use frozen fruits; they will need warming more gently to make sure they don't break down too much.

BREAD-CRUMBS & CROUTONS

No bread should ever be wasted – especially when you have made it with your own hands. Breadcrumbs are a great way to use up any surplus. Fresh or dry, they can be used for toppings, for coating, to bind, to stuff and even in sauces. Croutons (big breadcrumbs, if you like) are a brilliant addition to any soup or salad, adding flavour and texture.

MAKING BREADCRUMBS

There's really no need to buy breadcrumbs. Crusts and ends of bread can be stored in a bag in the freezer until you build up enough to turn them into breadcrumbs. The bread doesn't even have to be white. Potato & rosemary bread (see page 50) makes almost instant stuffing, seasoned and ready to use.

To make crumbs, pop the bread into a food processor and blitz, or use the coarse side of a grater. Slightly stale bread works best. If you end up making more than you need, store them in a plastic bag in the freezer.

Or better still dry them out. Spread the crumbs on a baking tray and place in a low oven at 150°C (300°F/Gas 2) for 20 minutes, until golden and dry, stirring halfway through. Dry breadcrumbs will keep for several weeks in an airtight container.

MAKING CROUTONS

Cut the bread into rough cubes, season with salt and pepper and drizzle with olive oil. Spread over a baking tray and place in a low oven at 150°C (300°F/Gas 2). Bake for 20–25 minutes, until golden and crisp. They will keep for up to two weeks in an airtight container but are best eaten fresh.

RICH BUTTERY CROUTONS

Cut the bread into rough cubes and season. Put a little clarified butter (see page 95) in a frying pan and cook the croutons over a medium heat until evenly golden.

BREADCRUMBS
FOR ADDED CRUNCH
& TOPPINGS

Buttered breadcrumbs are fantastic on gratins and for topping casseroles and pasta bakes. Mixed with some shredded mozzarella they make an unbeatable topping for roasted peppers.

TOMATES PROVENCALES

This recipe is close to Duncan's heart — he remembers it being served by his family down in the south of France as a funky accompaniment to a Sunday roast. It'll make a great, unexpected addition to a meal and takes no time at all to put together — so bring a little sunshine into your life.

♠ Combine the breadcrumbs, garlic and herbs in a bowl. Add a drizzle of olive oil and mix so that the crumbs are evenly coated. Season with salt and pepper to taste.

♠ Preheat the oven to 200°C (400°F/Gas 6). Prepare the tomatoes by slicing off the tops and de-seeding them with a teaspoon to leave empty vessels ready for the filling.

♠ Fill each tomato with two heaped tablespoons of the breadcrumb mix and place on a baking tray. Add a final drizzle of olive oil and bake for 15–20 minutes, until the tomatoes are softened and the breadcrumbs golden.

Makes 8

150 g (5 ½ oz) breadcrumbs

3 garlic cloves, finely chopped

5 tsp dried mixed herbs

olive oil

8 fresh tomatoes

sea salt & freshly ground black pepper

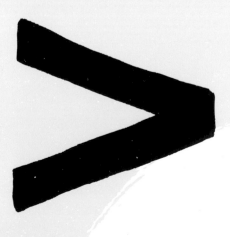

BREAD BAG

Hang a cotton shopping bag on the back of your kitchen or pantry door to store unused slices and crusts ready for breadcrumbing. The fabric allows air through so the bread will dry out without becoming mouldy.

BREADCRUMBS FOR CRUSTY COVERINGS

From fish and chicken fillets to kievs, scotch eggs and deep-fried camembert, breadcrumbs are a quick way to create a crisp, crunchy shell. Flour and egg bind the crumbs to the surface – follow the method for the fish below.

CRUNCHY COATED FISH WITH A LEMON BUTTER SAUCE

♠ Sprinkle the flour on to a large plate and season it with salt and pepper. Put the eggs in a bowl and the breadcrumbs on a second large plate or baking tray. Season the fish with sea salt. Dip each fillet first in the flour, shaking off the excess, and then in the egg. Finally, coat it in the breadcrumbs.

♠ When you are ready to fry, heat the olive oil in a frying pan over a medium heat. Lay the fillets in the pan, keeping them well spaced apart. Turn down the heat slightly and cook for four minutes, then turn over to fry the other side. Cooking times will vary depending on the thickness and type of fish. To check if the fish is cooked, push the tip of a knife gently into the thickest part of the fillet. If it feels hot when you remove it and place it on your lip, the fish is done.

♠ Remove the fish fillets from the pan and allow to rest while you quickly make the sauce. Add the butter to the same pan. As it starts to foam add a generous squeeze of lemon juice and a pinch of sea salt. Stir together and serve drizzled over the fish.

Serves 2

4 tbsp plain (all-purpose) flour

2 eggs, lightly beaten

150 g (5 ½ oz) breadcrumbs

2 white fish fillets, skin removed

3 tbsp olive oil

50 g (1 ¾ oz) butter

1 lemon

sea salt & freshly ground black pepper

BREADCRUMBS FOR STUFFING & BINDING

Serves 4

3 tsp olive oil

1 banana shallot, finely chopped

50 g (1¾ oz) butter

2 dessert apples, peeled, cored and diced

3 tsp finely chopped sage

200 g (7 oz / 3⅓ cups) breadcrumbs

sea salt & freshly ground black pepper

With onion and herbs in a traditional stuffing, or mixed with mozzarella cheese in courgette (zucchini) flowers, breadcrumbs make a delicious filling. Alternatively, use them to bind meatballs and Thai crab cakes.

APPLE & SAGE STUFFING

♠ You can use white breadcrumbs, but if you happen to have some made from either potato & rosemary or sage & onion bread (see page 50), even better.

♠ Warm the oil in a frying pan over a medium heat. Cook the shallot until soft and tender but not browned. Add the butter to the pan and once melted stir in the apple and sage.

♠ Add the cooked shallot and apple mixture to the breadcrumbs. Mix together and season.

♠ You can use this stuffing in meat or vegetables. Patrick likes simply to spread it across a baking tray and place it in the oven for 10–15 minutes at 180°C (350°F/Gas 4) along with the Sunday roast, until warmed through and crispy on top.

BREADCRUMBS AS THICKENING FOR SAUCES

BREAD SAUCE

★ This is a sauce Patrick's mother makes every Christmas – in fact it wouldn't be Christmas dinner without it. Every year the family all laugh when, like clockwork, she says: 'Oh I should make this more often, it's so easy.' It will still be 12 months before she does it again.

★ To make the sauce, first pour the milk into a saucepan. Stud the onion with the cloves and add it to the milk along with the bay leaf, peppercorns and salt.

★ Bring the milk to a gentle simmer then turn the heat right down. Cover with a lid and leave on a very gentle heat to infuse for at least an hour – longer if you have the time.

★ Strain the milk into a clean pan and add the breadcrumbs. Cook for 10 minutes, stirring occasionally, until thick. Just before serving stir in the butter. Check the seasoning and finish with some grated nutmeg. Pour into a sauce boat and serve.

Serves 6

1 litre (35 fl oz / 4 cups) milk

1 onion, peeled

8–10 cloves

1 bay leaf

1 tsp white peppercorns

2 tsp sea salt

300 g (10 ½ oz) breadcrumbs

2 tbsp butter

a little grated nutmeg, to taste

LITTLE MISS PIGGY

OUR LITTLE BLACK BOOK

We thought we would share some names and numbers of places we use to source our ingredients and equipment, as well as links to information, courses and more.

EQUIPMENT

The Thoughtful Bread Company
It would be criminal not to give ourselves a plug, given that we are developing a following among keen Real Bread home bakers. We offer a range of products that we use ourselves in the bakery for you to make use of when baking at home.
www.thethoughtfulbreadcompany.com

BAKERY BITS
For any artisan baking kit that we don't stock, these are the guys to go to.
bakerybits.co.uk

NISBETS
We buy our other general bakery or cooking kit from Nisbets. Not the most exciting, but they stock pretty much everything and with free delivery, you'll get a good price.
www.nisbets.co.uk

FLOUR

SHIPTON MILL
We buy the bulk of our flour from Shipton Mill, based in the West Country. There are a multitude of good mills producing high-quality flour who will do mail order or stock somewhere local to you, but we couldn't get away without mentioning Shipton for the support they have given us and the quality of the flour they produce, which is second to none.
www.shipton-mill.com

WESSEX MILL
We buy our six-seed flour and a fantastic granary flour called Wessex Cobber from them.
www.wessexmill.co.uk

SHARPHAM PARK
For all things spelt, these are the people.
www.sharphampark.com

SALT

You want to buy decent sea salt, and in Britain there are a handful of really good producers.

CORNISH SEA SALT CO
www.cornishseasalt.co.uk

HALEN MÔN
www.halenmon.com

MALDON SEA SALT COMPANY
This is a slight exception, as Maldon salt is harvested from the Blackwater estuary, the saltiest river in Britain, fed by the sea. This high-grade salt is revered by chefs worldwide.
www.maldonsalt.co.uk

GROWING YOUR OWN

DARTMOOR CHILLI FARM
To grow your own chillies, as we do, try Dartmoor Chilli Farm. They ship both live plants and seeds and have been a huge help in allowing us to set up our own chilli factory in our geodome.
www.dartmoorchillifarm.co.uk

GEO-DOME
If you want to have a mini Eden Project of your very own then, like us, you can! Paul, who runs Geo-Dome, is a skilled craftsman who builds geodomes by hand in varying sizes to suit space requirements and budget.
www.geo-dome.co.uk

INFORMATION

REAL BREAD CAMPAIGN
These guys are at the forefront of the campaign for Real Bread (which is what we make, in contrast to the commercial stuff). For links to bread-making courses, an interactive Real Bread stockists finder and educational resources, check them out.
www.realbreadcampaign.org

BLOGS, BOOKS & FORUMS

www.danlepard.com/forum
www.thefreshloaf.com/forum
www.wildyeastblog.com/
www.cookingbread.com/

Dough and Crust by Richard Bertinet
The Handmade Loaf by Dan Lepard
Bread Matters by Andrew Whitley
Bourke Street Bakery by Paul Allam and David McGuiness

INDEX

ABOUT
THE AUTHORS

PATRICK RYAN

Born in Ireland, the youngest of five, Patrick was
the 'black sheep' of the family. He has a degree in
corporate law, but swapped legal books for chef's
knives after a summer in Greece, going on to win awards
and work at Michelin-starred restaurants. A year's travel
included South America, New Zealand and Australia,
and a while with Tribewanted in Fiji — where his path
crossed with Duncan's. After some wining and dining by
Duncan, he agreed to move to Bath and be head baker of
The Thoughtful Bread Company, bringing his passion and
expertise, and developing its prize-winning recipes.
He and Duncan have also helped to set up a community
bakery in the Yorkshire Dales.

DUNCAN GLENDINNING

Originally from London, and with a French mother,
Duncan started his career as a web developer in Bath.
But he soon picked up a trowel and began to grow his
own vegetables. He ended up featuring on *It's Not
Easy Being Green* (BBC2) and later travelled to Fiji
as a sustainability worker for the unique eco-tourism
project Tribewanted. Back in the UK, he was inspired
to begin his own venture, with a strong environmental
and sustainable angle. His eureka moment came when
making bread for friends — he realised that it is one
of the rare universal foodstuffs. In 2009 he founded
The Thoughtful Bread Company, also contributing his
skills for foraging and thrifty sourcing.

ACKNOWLEDGEMENTS

We would like to thank everyone who had a hand in helping make this book become a reality. Caroline and Clive from Harris + Wilson, and everyone at our publisher Murdoch Books, for taking a chance on us. Designers Ross, Alex and Olly from A-Side Studio, photographer Jonathan Cherry and video guru James Aiken, for bringing the book to life, and Jane Middleton for her invaluable editorial contribution.

For all those who helped to give this book life and personality, this is a huge thank you from us both. Aaron, Will, Barry, Pete, Woody and Ross — we couldn't have found more eager taste testers. To Laura, Ash, Emily, Julia and Becks for adding a much-needed touch of beauty. To Rob, Sam and Claire a special thank you for allowing us invade your homes. To all the staff and kids at Farrington Gurney Primary School — your smiles and creativity are an inspiration.

We would like to take this opportunity to thank a few friends of Thoughtful Bread who have been with us since the beginning, supplying us with high-quality ingredients and support. Alan and all those at Shipton Mill; John and The Cheddar Gorge Cheese Company — your cheese is unrivalled; Fussels — the best rapeseed oil in the south-west if you ask us; Paul Robinson from Geo-Dome and Phil Palmer from Dartmoor Chilli Farm; and all the guys at Bath Pig — here's to a successful future. Also the Pump Room, Demuths, Prior Park Garden Centre and The Chequers, the very first wholesale customers to believe in our products.

All those at Farrington's Farm Shop, the best neighbours a bakery could have. Andy and Tish for putting a roof over the head of Thoughtful Bread. Also to Will Rich from ARB Environmental and Paul and his shotgun — it was the most fun we have ever had with a loaf of bread.

And a heartfelt thank-you to all our regular customers for their loyalty — without you The Thoughtful Bread Company wouldn't be what it is today.

'I would like to personally thank my team — Patrick, Andy, Ross, Nicola, Tim, James and Andrew at Thoughtful Bread — who work tirelessly and often under immense pressure to make things happen. To Patrick, mastermind of our very many recipes, which are a true signature of our success — good job, man. And to Rob, who spent many a long day and night with me thrashing out the ins and outs of the business before it was even born — I couldn't have done it without you. To friends and family, often neglected through the long hours, for not disowning me! Finally, I wouldn't be who I am today, and the business wouldn't be the success it is, had it not been for the unequivocal support and encouragement of my wife, Julia, whom I love so dearly. Thank you for being there for me.'
Duncan Glendinning

'I would like to take this opportunity to personally thank all my friends and especially my family — the world would be a very lonely place without you. I never thought the day would come when I would find myself writing a book, so for all those who have inspired me, believed in me and who I have had the opportunity to break bread with, thank you! Duncan — we have come a long way from the whiskey and cigars shared on a beach in Fiji to where we are today, you should be very proud. And finally to Laura, you have been by my side throughout this entire journey, early mornings, late nights — you have had to put up with it all. Thank you for not giving up on me.'
Patrick Ryan

A special mention to all our recipe testers — you have helped give strength to all our recipes: Patrick's mum, Elaine, Anna, Chris, Niamhai, Trisha, Margaret, Mammy Moore, Shui, Carl, Claire W, Claire J and Kris, Jessica, Jules, Tony, Jill, Amy, Urvashi, Amanda, Rich.

The
Thoughtful
BREAD CO

Open:
Tues-Fri, 9am - 6pm
Saturdays, 8am - 2pm

Handcrafted, Earth-Friendly

Ring the bakery: 01761 452806
Visit our website: www.thethoughtfulbreadcompany.com

BARTERING

THE
THOUGHTFUL
BREAD CO

Delicious EATS and
Summertime TREATS including
award-winning REAL BREADS,
pastries, cheese, chorizo,
chutneys & jams.

Come and have a Nibble!

Published in 2012 by **Murdoch Books Pty Limited**

Murdoch Books Australia
Pier 8/9
23 Hickson Road
Millers Point NSW 2000
Phone: +61 (0) 2 8220 2000
Fax: +61 (0) 2 8220 2558
www.murdochbooks.com.au
info@murdochbooks.com.au

Murdoch Books UK Limited
Erico House
6th Floor
93–99 Upper Richmond Road
Putney, London SW15 2TG
Phone: +44 (0) 20 8785 5995
www.murdochbooks.co.uk
info@murdochbooks.co.uk

For Corporate Orders & Custom Publishing please contact:
In the UK, Christine Jones, Sales and Marketing Director
In Australia, Noel Hammond, National Business Development Manager

Publisher: **Sally Webb**
Publishing Manager – Food: **Anneka Manning**
Designed by: **A-Side Studio**
Photography: **Jonathan Cherry**
Project Editor: **Caroline Harris**
Recipe Consultant: **Jane Middleton**
Project Editor (Murdoch Books): **Claire Grady**
Production: **Joan Beal**
Created by: **Harris + Wilson**

National Library of Australia Cataloguing-in-Publication entry

Author: Glendinning, Duncan.
Title: Bread revolution : rise up and bake / Duncan Glendinning and Patrick Ryan.
ISBN: 9781742666686 (hbk.)
Notes: Includes index.
Subjects: Cooking (Bread).
Other Authors/Contributors: Ryan, Patrick.
Dewey Number: 641.815

A catalogue record for this book is available from the British Library.

Printed in 2012 by **C&C Offset**, China.

OVEN GUIDE: You may find cooking times vary depending on the oven you are using.
For fan-forced ovens, as a general rule, set the oven temperature to 20°C (35°F)
lower than indicated in the recipe.

TERMS AND MEASURES: We have used 15 ml (3 teaspoon) tablespoon measures in
this book. If you are using a 20 ml (4 teaspoon) tablespoon, for most recipes
the difference will not be noticeable. However, for recipes using baking powder,
bicarbonate of soda (baking soda) or small amounts of flour reduce the quantity
by a teaspoon for each tablespoon specified. We have used a 250 ml cup.